The
Ghosts,
Witches &
Vampires
Quiz Book
by
Arthur Liebman

ILLUSTRATED BY
JACK WILLIAMS

Library of Congress Cataloging-in-Publication Data

Liebman, Arthur, 1926–
    The ghosts, witches & vampires quiz book / Arthur Liebman ;
illustrated by Jack Williams.
      p.   cm.
    Includes index.
    Summary: Two dozen multiple choice quizzes about every type of
supernatural creature on TV, and in films, literature, myth, and
legend.
    ISBN 0-8069-8408-2
    1. Supernatural—Miscellanea.   2. Supernatural in literature—
Miscellanea.   3. Supernatural in motion pictures—Miscellanea.
[1. Supernatural—Miscellanea.]   I. Title.   II. Title: The ghosts,
witches, and vampires quiz book.
BF1040.L54   1991
001.9′44—dc20   91-23371
                                                      CIP
                                                       AC

10   9   8   7   6   5   4   3   2   1

Text © 1991 by Arthur Liebman
Illustrations © 1991 by Jack Williams
Published by Sterling Publishing Company, Inc.
387 Park Avenue South, New York, N.Y. 10016
Distributed in Canada by Sterling Publishing
% Canadian Manda Group, P.O. Box 920, Station U
Toronto, Ontario, Canada M8Z 5P9
Distributed in Great Britain and Europe by Cassell PLC
Villiers House, 41/47 Strand, London WC2N 5JE, England
Distributed in Australia by Capricorn Link Ltd.
P.O. Box 665, Lane Cove, NSW 2066
Manufactured in the United States of America
All rights reserved

Sterling ISBN 0-8069-8408-2 Trade

For Joyce
   who has held my hand
      so many times through so many encounters
          with
        various vampires
         assorted aliens
           and miscellaneous monsters

CONTENTS

Introduction

Welcome to THE GHOSTS, WITCHES & VAMPIRES QUIZ BOOK, a volume designed to entertain, amuse and inform. Its contents are based upon one of the most fascinating and engrossing aspects of popular culture—the universal interest in the supernatural.

Readers of classical literature and contemporary fiction will find many questions based upon the treatment of the macabre and paranormal by important authors of both past and present. They will find the terrifying creatures (and terrified heroines) of popular short stories and novels, and historical tyrants, whose monstrous deeds earned them a gory niche in the hall of infamy.

Shakespeare, of course, merits a quiz of his own. The creator of the most well known ghosts and witches in world literature is represented in this volume by a curious collection of questions surveying the Bard at his bloodiest best.

Devotees of Dickens, Poe, Shelley and Hawthorne will be challenged to recall characters, scenes and incidents from the works of the masters, as well as highlights from other works of mystery fiction, ranging from the popular Gothic novels of the 19th century to the best-selling works of Stephen King and other purveyors of contemporary fright.

Phantoms, witches and monsters drawn from myth and legend are perennial figures of interest in Western civilization. They are dealt with extensively in this volume, with many questions designed to reflect the continuing fascination with these fanciful and frightening subjects.

Those interested in the strange and unknown will be grimly delighted to find questions drawn from the epic poetry of Homer, the history of ancient Egypt with its mummies, tombs and arcane writings, and the folklore of Eastern Europe in which vampires, werewolves and other ghostly figures abound.

A major portion of this book is devoted to alien monsters, man-made oddities and assorted curious creatures that millions have come to fear and love in the current crop of Hollywood horror. Indeed, many readers may consider themselves most expert in answering this ghoulish group of questions that deal with poltergeists and predators, and, of course, demonic toys and inanimate objects that spring to life to thrill their popcorn-munching public. In addition, a wide representation of current horror films, cult classics, and low budget horror films of the 50s and 60s that have earned film immortality—or notoriety— has been included to evoke chills, nostalgia or amusement.

Fans of the black-and-white monster films of the 30s and 40s— those films that pioneered and defined the horror genre—will have their recollections stimulated as they try to recall the actors and actresses who played Dracula, Frankenstein and the other monsters, as well as the madmen and maidens in films that have become part of international folklore, whose creatures have been transformed over the years from figures of unspeakable evil to heroes of popular affection— lovable and sympathetic beings fit to adorn sweatshirts and breakfast cereal boxes.

This volume of multiple choice questions indeed assembles an all-star cast of the ghostly and ghastly to test your puzzle solving mettle: villainous vampires, wailing werewolves, flying lizards, and sinister scientists are all here in featured roles. And, of course, mutant insects, entities and blobs who have crawled, crept or oozed themselves into our affections are also to be found among the delightful denizens who await you here.

I
DRACULA &
FRANKENSTEIN

1. Yes, There Was a Dracula

1. The word "Transylvania" means "_____."

    A   dark land   C   mountain home

    B   land beyond the forest   D   rushing waters

2. In various Balkan dialects, the name "Dracula" means "_____."

    A   child of the storm   C   son of the dragon

    B   son of the monster   D   son of the night

3. The historical Dracula was a ruler of a part of Romania called _____.

    A   Borodina   C   Lugara

    B   Wallachia   D   Vambrey

4. The historical Dracula was known as _____ to his people.

    A   Kara Dracula   C   Lugos Dracula

    B   Soni Dracula   D   Vlad Dracula

5. A famous picture of the historical Dracula shows him _____ while surrounded by many corpses.

    A   sleeping   C   dancing

    B   feasting   D   smiling

6. Historically, the name "Dracula" was applied to _____.

    A   all Romanian noblemen
    B   all wise and just leaders
    C   various members of a Romanian ruling family
    D   all heroes who died in battle

7. The historical Dracula lived from approximately_____.

    A   1510–1574   C   1320–1399
    B   1430–1476   D   1399–1452

8. According to the many 15th and 16th century stories about Dracula, his favorite method of executing his enemies was _____.

    A   strangulation   C   hanging
    B   beheading   D   impaling them upon stakes

9. According to various historical sources, the real Dracula killed more than _____ people in the Transylvania district of Sibiu.

    A   5,000   C   3,000
    B   10,000   D   400

10. In many parts of the Balkans, Dracula is viewed as a hero because he defended Christianity in wars against the _____.

    A   Russians   C   Germans
    B   Turks   D   Egyptians

11. Unlike the popular image of Dracula, the historical Dracula had

_____.

    A   only one eye   C   a long beard
    B   a deformed left arm   D   a large moustache

12. According to a number of historical sources, the real Dracula
    _____.

    A   drowned a thousand children in one day
    B   nailed turbans to the heads of his enemies
    C   set fire to the largest church in Romania
    D   poisoned two thousand people at a state dinner

13. Today, tourists may visit _____ Castle in Transylvania,
    which may have been the home of the real Dracula.

    A   Klop   C   Zog
    B   Bran   D   Buda

14. Which statement is *not* true about Bram Stoker, the author of the
    novel *Dracula*?

    A   He was the first to link the historical Dracula with the
    vampire legends.
    B   He wrote two other Dracula novels.
    C   He was born in Ireland.
    D   He was a friend of Mark Twain and Oscar Wilde.

15. Which statement is true about the methods used by Bram Stoker
    to research the material for his novel *Dracula*?

    A   He visited Transylvania.
    B   He did his research in London's British Museum.
    C   He travelled throughout Europe investigating vampire
    traditions.
    D   He interviewed descendants of the real Dracula.

16. While on a visit to America, Bram Stoker visited _____,
    whom he admired very much.

    A   President Theodore Roosevelt
    B   Andrew Carnegie
    C   Walt Whitman
    D   Jack London

17. Dracula's castle was located in Transylvania, near the _____ Pass.

   A   Burgo   C   Grodni
   B   Karga   D   Tula

18. _____ Abbey was the mysterious house in London rented by Count Dracula.

   A   Gotham   C   Carfax
   B   Landsdown   D   Tudor

19. In the novel *Dracula*, the ship that brought Dracula to England docked at _____.

   A   Whitby   C   Manchester
   B   London   D   Cornwall

20. In the novel *Dracula*, Count Dracula took _____ coffins to London.

   A   20   C   50
   B   10   D   3

2. Transylvania Mania

1. In the novel *Dracula*, Count Dracula tells _____ of his family's distinguished but bloody history as rulers of Transylvania.

   A   Jonathan Harker   C   Dr. Van Helsing
   B   Renfield   D   Dr. Seward

2. In Bram Stoker's novel, Count Dracula appears _____ in the daytime.

   A   at a concert   C   at the London Zoo
   B   on a train   D   in a museum

3. According to Transylvania traditions, a necklace of _____ worn around the neck may be used to ward off a vampire.

   A   seaweed   C   wheat
   B   rose vines   D   garlic

4. Which of the following is not the name of a character in Bram Stoker's novel *Dracula*?

   A   Jonathan Harker   C   Lucy Westerna
   B   Dr. John Seward   D   Martin Gore

5. The unusual thing about Dracula's hands was the fact that
_____.

   A he had six fingers
   B his nails were black
   C he had hair growing on his palms
   D his thumb was misshapen

6. Count Dracula could gain admission to a house only if he
_____.

   A was invited to enter
   B entered through a window
   C appeared on a moonlit night
   D was called by a beautiful woman

7. Renfield, the character in *Dracula* who loved to eat insects, was
called _____.

   A a draconius   C a verminian
   B an insectorian   D a zoophagus

8. _____ is the name of a brave American who helps hunt
down Dracula in Bram Stoker's novel.

   A Robert Hudson   C Ned Washington
   B Quincey Morris   D John Brown

9. The original movie version of *Dracula* starred Bela Lugosi, whose
real name was _____.

   A Karim Sin   C Bela Krantz
   B Bela Ludvoki   D Bela Blasko

10. Bela Lugosi was born in the Hungarian town of _____ in
1882.

   A Lugos   C Borga
   B Belat   D Lucarno

11. In the final pages of the novel *Dracula*, the Count is killed by
_____.

    A   a stake driven through his heart
    B   being stabbed through the heart with a Bowie knife
    C   the rays of a rising sun
    D   having his head cut off

12. For many years, Bram Stoker, the creator of Dracula, was
_____.

    A   a member of Parliament
    B   stage manager for the great British actor, Sir Henry
        Irving
    C   an advisor to Queen Victoria
    D   a distinguished soldier

13. After the opening scenes of the film *Dracula*, most of the action
takes place in _____.

    A   Cairo   C   Paris
    B   New York   D   London

14. "The children of the night, what _____ they make," is a
famous line spoken by Bela Lugosi as Count Dracula.

    A   dreams   C   wonders
    B   music   D   beautiful sounds

15. The name of the scientist who finally destroyed Dracula is
_____.

    A   Dr. Warner   C   Dr. Karis
    B   Professor Linden   D   Dr. Van Helsing

16. _____ played the female lead opposite Bela Lugosi in
Dracula.

    A   Mae Marsh   C   Fay Wray
    B   Helen Chandler   D   Evelyn Ankers

17. _____ played the part of Renfield in Bela Lugosi's *Dracula*.

    A Lon Chaney, Jr.   C Dwight Frye
    B George Zucco   D Glen Strange

18. Bela Lugosi's film *Dracula* was based, for the most part, on _____.

    A Bram Stoker's novel *Dracula*
    B Hamilton Dean's stage play *Dracula*
    C old Hungarian legends
    D historical records of Count Dracula

19. _____ directed Bela Lugosi in his immortal performance in *Dracula*.

    A Val Lewton   C Curt Siodmak
    B Frank Capra   D Tod Browning

20. Before making the film, Bela Lugosi played the role of Dracula on the Broadway stage in _____.

    A 1923   C 1924
    B 1927   D 1930

3. Draculas by the Dozen

1. The first important English vampire story, "The Vampyre" by John Polidori, was suggested by the image of _____.

   A   Lord Byron   C   Sir Richard Burton
   B   The Duke of Wellington   D   Sir Francis Drake

2. In John Polidori's story "The Vampyre," the name of the vampire is

   _____.

   A   Lord Frederick   C   Lord Carfax
   B   Lord Ruthven   D   Sir Rodney Lee

3. Lon Chaney played the role of a vampire in the first major Hollywood production of a film about vampires called

   _____.

   A   *The Next Corner*   C   *The Tower of Lies*
   B   *London After Midnight*   D   *West of Zanzibar*

4. In the classic German silent film *Nosferatu*, the name of the baldheaded, long-fanged vampire was Count _____.

   A   Orlock   C   Yorga
   B   Karla   D   Adrak

5. In the German silent film *Nosferatu*, the vampire was killed by
   _____.

   A   the first rays of the rising sun
   B   a sharp knife
   C   a wooden stake
   D   the rays of the moon

6. Most of the action in the 1943 film *The Son of Dracula* took place
   in the mysterious house known as _____.

   A   Dark Oaks   C   Tatter Hill
   B   Night Shade   D   Fogbound

7. In the 1943 film *The Son of Dracula*, Count Dracula assumed the
   name of Count _____.

   A   Cardalu   C   Alucard
   B   Radac   D   Cularda

8. _____ played the role of Count Dracula in *The House of
   Frankenstein*.

   A   John Carradine   C   Lionel Atwill
   B   David Manners   D   George Zucco

9. _____, the author of *Sweeney Todd*, was the author of
   Varney the Vampire, a novel published many years before *Dracula*.

   A   Wilkie Collins   C   Horace Walpole
   B   Thomas Paine   D   Thomas Prest

10. Which one of the following has *not* played Dr. Van Helsing in a
    vampire movie?

    A   Sir Laurence Olivier   C   Edward Van Sloan
    B   Gregory Peck   D   Peter Cushing

11. In *The Son of Dracula*, Dracula was played by _____.

    A   Lionel Atwill   C   Lon Chaney, Jr.

    B   Wallace Ford   D   George Brent

12. Which one of these *Dracula* pictures took place in America?

    A   *Dracula's Daughter*   C   *The House of Dracula*

    B   *Dracula*   D   *The Son of Dracula*

13. A Roman Polanski film about vampires, starring Sharon Tate, was called _____.

    A   *Count Yorga*

    B   *The Fearless Vampire Killers*

    C   *Monster, Go Home*

    D   *The Night Walker*

14. _____ was a very handsome Count Dracula in a TV miniseries.

    A   Kirk Douglas   C   David Niven

    B   Rock Hudson   D   Louis Jourdan

15. *Love at First Bite* starred _____ as a romantic Dracula.

    A   Vincent Price   C   George Hamilton

    B   Robert Redford   D   Alan Alda

16. *Old Dracula* presented the Count as a bloody senior citizen. Who played the title role?

    A   Melvyn Douglas   C   Ricardo Montalban

    B   David Niven   D   Louis Jourdan

17. The sexy hostess of the TV series *Shock Theatre*, was featured in a few Hollywood horror films. Her name was _____.

    A   Draculesse   C   Sylvania

    B   The Countess   D   Vampira

18. At the end of the Bela Lugosi *Dracula* film, an actor appeared on the screen to tell the audience _____.

    A   "Sleep well tonight; vampires do not exist"
    B   "Beware if you don't see your image in a mirror"
    C   "If you hear wings flapping, don't open your window"
    D   "There are such things"

19. Christopher Lee did *not* play the Count in _____.

    A   *The Scar of Dracula*   C   *Dracula's Daughter*
    B   *Dracula A.D. 1972*   D   *Taste the Blood of Dracula*

20. According to tradition, which of the following methods may *not* be used to destroy a vampire?

    A   Drive a stake through its heart.
    B   Crush the vampire with rocks.
    C   Chop off the head.
    D   Burn the corpse.

4. Frankenstein: the Novel

1. Mary Shelley, the author of *Frankenstein*, lived from
   _____ .

   A 1883–1934   C 1788–1830
   B 1797–1851   D 1810–1879

2. Mary Shelley's father was the famous British philosopher and
   novelist _____ .

   A William Godwin   C John Stuart Mill
   B Jeremy Fox   D David Hume

3. Which statement about the first edition of *Frankenstein* is true?

   A The author's name was not revealed.
   B It was published in French.
   C It was banned by the church.
   D It was printed in red ink.

4. Letters written by _____ are important elements in the
   plot of *Frankenstein*.

   A Russell, a scientist
   B Walton, a sea captain
   C Williams, a young student
   D Lessing, a famous painter

5. The complete title of Mary Shelley's novel is *Frankenstein: The Modern* _____.

    A *God*   C *Monster*

    B *Prometheus*   D *Zeus*

6. Mary Shelley was about _____ years old when she wrote the novel *Frankenstein*.

    A 30   C 24

    B 19   D 45

7. *Frankenstein* was first published in _____.

    A 1840   C 1930

    B 1816   D 1888

8. In the novel *Frankenstein*, the monster kills _____.

    A   the bride of Dr. Frankenstein

    B   the father of Frankenstein

    C   a cruel police officer

    D   a wolf that attacked him

9. The opening scene of the novel *Frankenstein* takes place
_____.

   A   in a laboratory   C   on a mountain top
   B   near the North Pole   D   in an African jungle

10. Mary Shelley's mother was the famous woman philosopher and
pioneer feminist _____.

   A   Hannah Page   C   Elizabeth Barrett
   B   Elizabeth Bennett   D   Mary Wollstonecraft

11. In Mary Shelley's novel, the newly created creature is described as
follows: "His _____ skin scarcely covered the work of
muscles and arteries beneath."

   A   purple   C   charred
   B   yellow   D   green

12. Which is true of the monster in the novel?

   A   He learns to speak perfect English.
   B   He learns to paint portraits.
   C   He is a great admirer of Italian opera.
   D   He visits the British Museum.

13. In the novel *Frankenstein*, the monster describes his wish for a
bride as _____.

   A   "a creature more beautiful than any other female"
   B   "a creature as deformed as myself"
   C   "a creature of beauty to contrast my ugliness"
   D   "a bride of doom"

14. Frankenstein began making a mate for the monster in his laboratory in _____.

   A   Germany   C   Malta
   B   the Orkney Islands   D   Italy

15. Mary Shelley first conceived the idea for *Frankenstein* while visiting the villa of the famous English poet _____.

    A William Wordsworth   C John Keats

    B Lord Byron   D Samuel Taylor Coleridge

16. Which of the following great classics was *not* read by the monster in the novel?

    A *The Decline and Fall of the Roman Empire*

    B *Paradise Lost*

    C Goethe's *Sorrows of Werther*

    D *Candide*

17. "All men hate the wretched: how, then, must I be hated, who am miserable beyond all living things!" These lines are spoken by _____ in Mary Shelley's novel.

    A Dr. Frankenstein

    B the monster

    C the monster's bride

    D Frankenstein's cruel assistant

18. At the end of the novel, the monster _____.

    A   is killed by lightning
    B   disappears on an ice floe in the Arctic Ocean
    C   is crushed by falling rocks
    D   is destroyed by the villagers

19. In addition to *Frankenstein*, Mary Shelley wrote the imaginative novel _____.

    A   *The Castle of Otranto*   C   *Northanger Abbey*
    B   *The Last Man*   D   *Looking Backward*

20. _____ played the role of Mary Shelley, the author of the novel *Frankenstein*, in *The Bride of Frankenstein*.

    A   Elsa Lanchester   C   Frances Dee
    B   Evelyn Ankers   D   Miriam Hopkins

5. Frankenstein: the Films

1. The opening scene of the classic film *Frankenstein* takes place
   _____.

   A at a funeral
   B in a laboratory

   C in a schoolroom
   D on top of a mountain

2. The name of Dr. Frankenstein's cruel laboratory assistant was
   _____.

   A Fritz
   B Emile

   C Igor
   D Trask

3. In *The Son of Frankenstein*, Police Inspector Krogh had a(n)
   _____.

   A glass eye
   B artificial ear

   C wooden arm
   D broken spine

4. In *Frankenstein*, Dr. Frankenstein's laboratory was located in a
   _____.

   A deserted tower
   B dungeon

   C cabin in the woods
   D cave in a mountain

5. _____ played Dr. Frankenstein in the original *Frankenstein*.

    A   Colin Clive   C   Basil Rathbone
    B   David Manners   D   Leslie Howard

6. The picturesque village used as the setting of *Frankenstein* was originally built for the film _____.

    A   *The Big Parade*
    B   *All Quiet on the Western Front*
    C   *Way Down East*
    D   *Seventh Heaven*

7. In *The Bride of Frankenstein*, the monster is befriended by a _____.

    A   blind hermit   C   group of gypsies
    B   kind priest   D   beautiful woman

8. _____ helped Dr. Frankenstein create a bride for the monster.

    A   Dr. Mabuse   C   Dr. Cyclops
    B   Dr. Pretorious   D   Dr. Death

9. At the end of *The Bride of Frankenstein*, the monster was killed
_____.

    A by a magic bullet   C by an avalanche
    B in an explosion   D in a flood

10. Which statement is true about the bride of Frankenstein?

    A She could not move.   C She could not speak.
    B She loved the monster. D She had only one arm.

11. The last words spoken by the monster in *The Bride of Frankenstein*
were_____.

    A "not alive"   C "life bad…death good"
    B "rest, rest, rest"   D "we belong dead"

12. The role of Dr. Frankenstein's evil assistant was played by
_____.

    A Leon Bradford   C Burke Owens
    B Carlon Paige   D Dwight Frye

13. The original *Frankenstein* was directed by _____.

    A Tod Browning   C James Whale
    B D.W. Griffith   D Joseph Von Sternberg

14. In *The Son of Frankenstein*, Frankenstein's son was named
_____.

    A Eric Frankenstein   C Alfred von Frankenstein
    B Karl von Frankenstein   D Wolfe von Frankenstein

15. _____ played the role of the horrible Igor in a number of
Frankenstein films.

    A Dwight Frye   C Glen Strange
    B Lon Chaney, Jr.   D Bela Lugosi

16. Who was not killed by the monster in the original film *Frankenstein*?

    A   Frankenstein's mother
    B   Fritz, Frankenstein's assistant
    C   a little girl
    D   Dr. Waldman, Frankenstein's teacher

17. Bela Lugosi was first offered the role of Frankenstein's monster, but refused it because _____.

    A   he wanted to play in a comedy
    B   he did not believe the picture would be a success
    C   he did not get a large raise after his success in *Dracula*
    D   the monster had no dialogue

18. _____ played the role of Dr. Frankenstein in *Young Frankenstein*.

    A   Bob Hope   C   Mel Brooks
    B   Gene Wilder   D   Marty Feldman

19. An X-rated version of *Frankenstein* was made by _____.

    A   Francis Ford Coppola   C   Peter Bogdanovich
    B   Andy Warhol   D   Peyton Shaw

20. At the end of *The Ghost of Frankenstein*, the monster and the Wolf Man were _____.

    A   hanged   C   electrocuted
    B   drowned   D   buried in a deep tomb

II
CLASSIC MOVIE
MONSTERS

6. King Kong

1. _____ played the role of the beautiful blonde whom King Kong carried to the top of the Empire State Building.

    A   Fay Wray
    B   Helen Chandler

    C   Thelma Todd
    D   Evelyn Ankers

2. All of these prehistoric creatures except the _____ appeared in *King Kong*.

    A   stegosaurus
    B   apatosaurus

    C   sabre tooth tiger
    D   pterandon

3. King Kong was finally captured on his island by the movie crew who used _____ to subdue him.

    A   gas bombs
    B   nets

    C   sleeping pills
    D   a gigantic trap

4. In *King Kong*, Kong was described by the man who captured him as _____.

    A   "the eighth wonder of the world"
    B   "the master of mankind"
    C   "the giant of giants"
    D   "the master of monsters"

5. King Kong was captured on _____.

    A   Terror Island   C   Skull Island
    B   Magic Island   D   Mystic Island

6. In the film the name of the movie producer who captured and exploited King Kong was _____.

    A   Lou Shaw   C   Carl Denham
    B   Mark Harris   D   Louis Lord

7. King Kong was killed _____.

    A   climbing a mountain
    B   as he ran through the jungle
    C   on the top of the Empire State Building
    D   by a subway train

8. *King Kong* ended with one of the most famous last lines in movie history: "It was _____ that killed the beast."

    A   beauty   C   love
    B   mankind   D   science

9. _____, the composer of the music for *Gone With the Wind*, composed the excellent movie score for the original *King Kong*.

    A   Alfred Newman   C   Hans Eisler
    B   Miklos Roza   D   Max Steiner

10. _____ created the image of King Kong in the film classic.

    A   Willis O'Brien   C   Louis Harrison
    B   Kent Shaw   D   Jack Pierce

11. In the 1976 color version of *King Kong*, Kong climbed up the _____.

    A   World Trade Center   C   Washington Monument
    B   Empire State Building   D   Eiffel Tower

12. In the 1976 version of *King Kong*, _____ was the girl in Kong's clutching hand.

    A   Jessica Lange   C   Cheryl Ladd
    B   Ingrid Pitt   D   Jill Clayburgh

13. _____ was the name of the ship that brought Kong to New York.

    A   Apollo   C   Venture
    B   Defiance   D   Marvel

14. In the original *King Kong*, the name of the girl that Kong fell in love with was _____.

    A   Ann Darrow   C   Joan Harris
    B   Laura Castle   D   Jane Lee

15. King Kong is called _____ in Japanese.

    A   Kingu Kongu   C   Kingalla
    B   Koto Kota   D   Kingatsu

16. Some of the prehistoric monsters in *King Kong* (1933) had appeared previously in a silent film entitled _____.

    A   *One Million B.C.*   C   *The Mysterious Island*
    B   *The Lost World*   D   *The Unknown Shore*

17. The world-famous writer of thrillers, _____, was given screen credit as a writer of the original *King Kong*.

    A   Sir Arthur Conan Doyle   C   Raymond Chandler
    B   Edgar Wallace   D   Edgar Rice Burroughs

18. In *King Kong* (1933) the name of the sea captain whose ship took the movie crew to King Kong's island was Captain _____.

    A   Volker   C   Sloan
    B   McDermott   D   Engelhorn

19. In the technicolor remake *King Kong* (1976) _____ struggled heroically to save the heroine from the clutches of the great ape.

    A   Jeff Bridges and Charles Grodin
    B   Beau Bridges and Rip Torn
    C   Keith Carradine and Donald Sutherland
    D   Richard Thomas and Jason Robards, Jr.

20. For the 1976 version of *King Kong*, Paramount Pictures constructed a robot ape _____ feet tall.

    A   100   C   128
    B   42   D   310

7. The Wolf Man & the Mummy

1. Complete the missing word from the classic "Wolf Man" poem:
   "Even a man who's pure at heart
   And says his prayers by night
   May become a wolf when the wolfbane blooms
   And the _____ moon is bright."

     A winter   C summer
     B autumn   D silver

2. _____ created the role of Wolf Man in 1941.

     A Boris Karloff   C Vincent Price
     B Bela Lugosi   D Lon Chaney, Jr.

3. The original *Wolf Man* film took place in _____.

     A the United States   C France
     B England   D Egypt

4. _____, who created the role of Charlie Chan, played a
   werewolf in *The Werewolf of London.*

     A Sidney Toler   C Charles Bickford
     B Warner Oland   D Wallace Ford

5. In *The Werewolf of London*, a scientist searched for a flower that bloomed _____.

    A   in a mysterious cave
    B   by the light of a full moon
    C   after the murder of a man
    D   once every hundred years

6. Which one of the following was an important element in the plot of *The Wolf Man*?

    A   a cane with a silver head
    B   a silver bullet
    C   a strange black cat
    D   a broken mirror

7. The name of the old gypsy woman in *The Wolf Man* was _____.

    A   Karala   C   Zora
    B   Maleva   D   Zeena

8. In *The Wolf Man*, the Wolf Man was killed by _____.

    A   the police   C   another wolf man
    B   his father   D   an elderly scientist

9. The name of the Wolf Man was _____.

    A   Fred Harris   C   Tony Smith
    B   Larry Talbot   D   Ralph Howard

10. _____ played the father of the Wolf Man in the original *Wolf Man* movie.

    A   Lionel Barrymore   C   Basil Rathbone.
    B   Claude Rains   D   Donald Crisp

11. The original *Mummy* film, *The Mummy* starring Boris Karloff, was made in _____.

    A   1932   C   1929

    B   1938   D   1937

12. In *The Mummy*, an Egyptian priest was kept alive for centuries by the priests of _____.

    A   Karnak   C   Tara-La

    B   Amtohop   D   Shar-i-to

13. In *The Mummy*, the scroll of _____ contained the secret of the Mummy's survival.

    A   Thoth   C   Karno

    B   La-Shi   D   Di-Bi-Ra

14. In the Boris Karloff film, the Mummy assumed the name _____ after he was reincarnated as a modern Egyptologist.

    A   Pasha Ray   C   Salib Kahn

    B   Ardath Bey   D   Mohandus Ka

15. According to Hollywood tradition, a mummy may be kept alive by the mysterious powers of _____ leaves.

    A   lotus   C   tana
    B   walpurgis   D   kara

16. In many of the later *Mummy* films, the name of the Mummy is _____.

    A   Kharis   C   Banas
    B   Zorta   D   Runus

17. In many *Mummy* films, the name of the Mummy's sweetheart was _____.

    A   Princess Ardela   C   Princess Ananka
    C   Corta-Ri   D   Donarta

18. _____ took place in Mapleton, Massachusetts.

    A   *The Mummy's Tomb*   C   *The Mummy's Curse*
    B   *The Mummy's Hand*   D   *The Mummy's Ghost*

19. *The Mummy's Hand*, *The Mummy's Tomb* and *The Mummy's Ghost* all featured _____.

    A   Lionel Atwill   C   George Zucco
    B   Otto Kruger   D   Basil Rathbone

20. _____ played the title role in the 1957 British technicolor film *The Mummy*.

    A   John Strange   C   Christopher Lee
    B   Peter Sellers   D   George Sanders

8. The Phantom of the Opera & the Hunchback of Notre Dame

1. The author of the novel *The Phantom of the Opera* is _____.

    A Gaston Leroux   C Bram Stoker
    B Victor Hugo   D Edgar Allan Poe

2. The name of the Phantom in *The Phantom of the Opera* was _____.

    A Martin   C Zoltan
    B Loris   D Eric

3. The Phantom of the Opera haunted a great opera house in _____.

    A London   C Paris
    B New York   D Rome

4. In *The Phantom of the Opera*, Lon Chaney's horrible face was suddenly revealed in a scene in which the Phantom was _____.

    A sleeping   C playing the organ
    B walking down a corridor D lighting a candle

5. One of Lon Chaney's greatest movie disguises was his makeup for the _____ sequence in *The Phantom of the Opera.*

    A   red death   C   guillotine
    B   flowing wine   D   spider

6. A _____ is an important property in most screen versions of *The Phantom of the Opera.*

    A   chandelier   C   mysterious painting
    B   stained glass window   D   Bible

7. Nelson Eddy appeared in the version of *The Phantom of the Opera* that starred _____ as the Phantom.

    A   Claude Rains   C   Spencer Tracy
    B   Vincent Price   D   Bela Lugosi

8. The 1962 English version of *The Phantom of the Opera* starred _____ in the title role.

    A   Christopher Lee   C   Herbert Lom
    B   Peter Cushing   D   Alec Guinness

9. In the novel *The Phantom of the Opera*, the young opera singer abducted by the Phantom is named _____.

   A   Christine   C   Cecile
   B   Marie   D   Claudette

10. In the novel *The Phantom of the Opera*, the Phantom composes a musical masterpiece entitled _____.

    A   "A Hero's Return"   C   "Overture to Glory"
    B   "Don Juan Triumphant"   D   "Paris by Moonlight"

11. The composer of the internationally hailed musical version of *The Phantom of the Opera* is _____.

    A   Jerry Herman   C   Andrew Lloyd Webber
    B   Jules Styne   D   Stephen Sondheim

12. After his silent film triumphs as the Phantom of the Opera and the Hunchback of Notre Dame, Lon Chaney made a triumphant transition to sound with an outstanding performance in

    _____.

    A   *The Unholy Three*   C   *The Bat*
    B   *Outside the Law*   D   *The Cat and the Canary*

13. The correct title of Victor Hugo's world-famous novel, which has become known as *The Hunchback of Notre Dame*, is

    _____.

    A   *Notre Dame of Paris*
    B   *The Church of Notre Dame*
    C   *The Towers of Notre Dame*
    D   *The Bells of Notre Dame*

14. Victor Hugo's novel about the Hunchback of Notre Dame was first published in _____.

    A   1880   C   1831
    B   1912   D   1862

15. The name of the Hunchback of Notre Dame was _____.

    A   Alucardo   C   Claudio

    B   Quasimodo   D   Varino

16. Lon Chaney's classic silent film *The Hunchback of Notre Dame*, was made in _____.

    A   1932   C   1923

    B   1921   D   1928

17. The Hunchback of Notre Dame fell in love with the gypsy girl because _____.

    A   she gave him a drink of water when he was being whipped

    B   she gave him a handkerchief

    C   she visited the bell tower with him

    D   she admired the large bells

18. In the Charles Laughton version of *The Hunchback of Notre Dame,* the gypsy girl was played by _____.

    A   Maureen O'Hara   C   Claire Trevor

    B   Lana Turner   D   Audrey Totter

19. The wicked master of the Hunchback of Notre Dame was

_____.

    A   Claude Frollo   C   George Grizelle

    B   Pierre Lamin   D   Casper Ruin

20. The only screen version of *The Hunchback of Notre Dame* to be made in France starred _____ in the title role.

    A   Charles Laughton   C   Anthony Quinn

    B   Lon Chaney, Jr.   D   Christopher Lee

9. Dr. Jekyll & the Invisible Man

1. The correct title of Robert Louis Stevenson's novel is
_____.

   A *The Horror of Dr. Jekyll and Mr. Hyde*
   B *The Adventures of Dr. Jekyll and Mr. Hyde*
   C *The Strange Case of Dr. Jekyll and Mr. Hyde*
   D *The Narrative of Dr. Jekyll and Mr. Hyde*

2. The author of *Dr. Jekyll and Mr. Hyde* is also the author of
_____.

   A *Treasure Island*   C *King Solomon's Mines*
   B *Ben Hur*   D *The Turn of the Screw*

3. In most versions of *Dr. Jekyll and Mr. Hyde*, Dr. Jekyll's transformation took place _____.

   A after drinking a potion
   B after a delicate operation
   C after being bitten by a wolf
   D only when there was no moon

4. _____ gave a fine performance in the 1920 silent movie version of *Dr. Jekyll and Mr. Hyde*.

   A John Barrymore   C Lon Chaney
   B Rudolph Valentino   D John Gilbert

5. Dr. Jekyll's first name was _____.

    A   James   C   Martin

    B   Jake   D   Henry

6. Mr. Hyde's first name was _____.

    A   Edward   C   Charles

    B   Lewis   D   Martin

7. At the end of the novel *Dr. Jekyll and Mr. Hyde*, the body of Dr. Jekyll was found _____.

    A   in his laboratory

    B   on a street corner

    C   in the dungeon of a castle

    D   in the attic of a museum

8. _____ won an Academy Award for his portrayal of Dr. Jekyll and Mr. Hyde.

    A   Fredric March   C   James Cagney

    B   Lon Chaney   D   Warner Baxter

9. Lana Turner and _____ both appeared in MGM's version of *Dr. Jekyll and Mr. Hyde*.

    A   Ingrid Bergman   C   Joan Crawford

    B   Joan Fontaine   D   Bette Davis

10. H.G. Wells' novel *The Invisible Man* was first published in _____.

    A   1870   C   1910

    B   1897   D   1900

11. The name of the Invisible Man was _____.

    A   Wallace   C   Griffin

    B   Caswell   D   Clayton

12. One of the most effective scenes in the original version of *The Invisible Man* was a scene in which _____.

    A a candle is cut in two
    B a cat is killed
    C bandages are removed
    D a goldfish is made invisible

13. In the original movie version, the Invisible Man was killed _____.

    A as he ran through the snow
    B in a blazing house
    C by a falling building
    D in a great explosion

14. _____ starred in the title role of the original *The Invisible Man*.

    A George Arliss   C Claude Rains
    B Paul Muni   D Warner Baxter

15. _____ played the Invisible Man in *The Invisible Man Returns*.

    A Vincent Price   C Brian Aherne
    B John Loder   D Louis Hayward

16. In H. G. Wells' novel, the Invisible Man rented a room in a country inn named the _____.

    A Royal George   C Fox and Hound
    B Coach and Horse   D Ink and Quill

17. *The Invisible Woman* starred _____ as an eccentric scientist.

    A Boris Karloff   C John Barrymore
    B Vincent Price   D Basil Rathbone

18. The *Topper* films and the *Topper* TV series featured
    _____, an invisible mischief-making married couple.

    A   Craig and Carol Doyle
    B   Ned and Nora Smith
    C   Hank and Mary Sloan
    D   George and Marion Kirby

19. _____ starred in a successful TV series entitled *The Invisible Man.*

    A   John Forsythe   C   William Shatner
    B   David McCallum   D   Richard Chamberlain

20. James Whale, the director of the classic film version of *The Invisible Man*, also directed the memorable musical film _____ in glorious black and white.

    A   *Naughty Marietta*   C   *Forty-Second Street*
    B   *Showboat*   D   *The Firefly*

10. Godzilla & Company

1. _____ starred in the original *Godzilla* film, *Godzilla: King of Monsters*.

    A   Charlton Heston   C   Raymond Burr
    B   Vincent Price   D   Adam West

2. In the original *Godzilla* film, Godzilla almost destroyed the city of _____.

    A   Tokyo   C   Singapore
    B   Manila   D   San Francisco

3. Godzilla was first discovered on _____ Island.

    A   Illata   C   Bika
    B   Karatu   D   Odo

4. At the end of *Godzilla*, the monster was apparently killed by _____.

    A   an atomic bullet   C   an oxygen destroyer
    B   a nuclear bomb   D   an atomic computer

5. *Son of Godzilla* featured Godzilla's cute little monster boy named
_____.

    A Luba   C Minya
    B Zaktar   D Golbut

6. Godzilla, Rodan and Mothra, three great movie monsters, ganged up to destroy Ghidrah, the fire-breathing dragon in
_____.

    A *Three-Headed Monster*   C *Monster Attack*
    B *Island of Monsters*   D *All My Monsters*

7. In *Godzilla Rides Again*, Godzilla waged a life and death struggle with the monstrous _____.

    A Gora   C Anzilla
    B Karazilla   D Rodan

8. In *Godzilla's Revenge*, Godzilla and his son fought against _____, the monster spider.

    A Spiega   C Motrata
    B Reptilious   D Spasita

9. The inhabitants of an undersea empire sent forth a monstrous insect to destroy civilization, but Godzilla came to the rescue in
_____.

    A *Battle of the Prehistoric Monsters*
    B *Godzilla's Revenge*
    C *Godzilla vs. Megalon*
    D *Godzilla vs. The Thing*

10. In _____, a giant caterpillar followed two girls to Japan, and then attacked Tokyo.

    A *Mothra*   C *Adrak*
    B *Azilla*   D *Mintors*

11. In the hysterical, historical epic _____, crazed alchemists in ancient Rome created an army of zombies to topple the empire.

   A *The War of the Zombies*   C *Zombies of Rome*
   B *Attack of the Zombies*   D *The White Zombie*

12. A giant octopus stopped traffic when he attacked the Golden Gate Bridge in _____.

   A *It Came from Beneath the Sea*
   B *Invasion of the Creature*
   C *It Conquered the World*
   D *Beast from 20,000 Fathoms*

13. A giant turtle and a flying beast that emitted poisoned smog engaged in a bloody struggle in _____.

   A *Monster from the Surf*
   B *Return of the Giant Monster*
   C *Godzilla vs. The Thing*
   D *They Came from Beyond Space*

14. In 1958, Steve McQueen faced the _____ in a life and death struggle.

    A   Creature   C   Monster Men
    B   Blob   D   Slime

15. A motherly monster destroyed a city while searching for a kidnapped child in _____.

    A   *While the City Sleeps*   C   *Gorgo*
    B   *Dead of Night*   D   *The Mole People*

16. Creatures from a flying saucer tried to dish up some trouble by reviving dead people and using them as zombies in _____.

    A   *War of the Colossal Beast*
    B   *Attack of the Zombies*
    C   *Plan Nine from Outer Space*
    D   *Man-Made Monster*

17. Giant insects attacked Los Angeles, but Los Angeles won the day in _____.

    A   *Five*   C   *We*
    B   *Killers*   D   *Them!*

18. In _____, a giant chicken, horrible honey bees and a tremendous crab attacked a group of Civil War soldiers.

    A   *Invasion of the Star Creatures*
    B   *Panic Island*
    C   *The Mysterious Island*
    D   *Voyage Into Death*

19. _____ began with a juicy scene indeed: a truckload of meat was hijacked by an ugly, hungry monster!

    A   *The Phantom of Blood Lake*
    B   *Attack of the Giant Leeches*
    C   *Ghost of Dragstrip Hollow*
    D   *War of the Colossal Beast*

20. A beautiful girl played the piano while held in the hands of a kindly monster in _____.

    A   *Godzilla*   C   *Mighty Joe Young*
    B   *Son of Kong*   D   *Reptilicus*

III
THE NEXT
GENERATION: ALIENS,
DEMONS & BLOBS

11. Gore Galore

1. Edward Scissorhands, a young man capable of some curious cut-ups, was welcomed by a kind lady who lived in _____.

    A   a trailer near Disneyland
    B   an apartment in Manhattan
    C   a house in the suburbs
    D   a ranch house near Santa Barbara

2. In *The Bride* (1985), a re-make of the classic *Bride of Frankenstein*, Frankenstein's monster goes into show business and becomes an outstanding _____.

    A   strong man   C   circus clown
    B   lion tamer   D   high wire acrobat

3. In *Ghost*, an awkward but friendly ghost who returned to earth to protect his girlfriend was played by _____.

    A   Tony Goldwin   C   Matthew Modine
    B   Aidan Quinn   D   Patrick Swayze

4. Tom Hanks' peaceful life in *The Burbs* was upset by some very unpleasant neighbors, the creepy _____ family.

    A   Kopek   C   Kessler
    B   Kramer   D   Karas

5. In the *Halloween* films, Donald Pleasence could always be relied upon to give a fine performance as the weird shrink _____.

   A Dr. Fortune   C Dr. Krieger
   B Dr. Dark   D Dr. Loomis

6. In *The Witches of Eastwick*, _____ played the delightful devil who cast his romantic spell over three women in Eastwick.

   A Jack Nicholson   C Emilio Estevez
   B Sam Sheppard   D Dan Ayckroyd

7. In *Back to the Future Part III*, Marty travels back to the year _____ to save Doc from the clutches of a beautiful woman.

   A 1984   C 1885
   B 1776   D 1492

8. Bill Cosby played the part of a father who _____, but returns from the next world as a friendly spirit to help his family.

   A gave his life to rescue a drowning child
   B was killed in an accident
   C was shot defending his family
   D died of lung cancer

9. A group of furry aliens cut some colorful capers _____ in *The Munchies*.

   A on a runaway school bus
   B in a bowling alley
   C on a miniature golf course
   D at a crowded shopping mall

10. In *Return of the Living Dead II*, the reappearance of the gruesome ghouls is brought about when three children _____.

    A   help a lonely—and seemingly harmless—stranger
    B   uncover a strange statue in an abandoned mine
    C   find a metal drum containing a strange gas
    D   look through an old book of macabre drawings

11. In *The Fog*, Jamie Lee Curtis plays a frightened resident of a small fishing village that is terrorized _____.

    A   by a swarm of mutant lobsters
    B   by ghosts of long-dead pirates
    C   by a strange gas that drives people mad
    D   by a gigantic land-crawling octopus

12. In *Little Shop of Horrors*, a young man is overwhelmed by a monster _____ that really drives him up the wall.

    A   goldfish   C   plant
    B   canary   D   kitten

13. In *Total Recall*, Arnold Schwarzenegger administers some hard-fisted justice when he takes on _____.

   A   a petty dictator
   B   the head of a large corporation
   C   an influential mob Godfather
   D   a group of newly arrived aliens

14. In *Arachnophobia*, a young Californian and his family are terrorized by a horde of horrible _____.

   A   spiders   C   ants
   B   rats   D   snakes

15. Stephen King's *Children of the Corn* deals with the gruesome adventures of _____.

   A   a family at Thanksgiving
   B   a travelling couple
   C   a platoon of soldiers
   D   a group of friendly aliens

16. In *Gremlins 2: The New Batch*, our furry friends follow their weirdo ways as they wreak havoc with a villainous _____.

   A   millionaire
   B   conceited movie director
   C   clever Russian spy
   D   family of psychotic killers

17. _____ played a tough Los Angeles cop, determined to destroy the predator who has been killing some of his police buddies.

   A   Eddie Murphy   C   Danny Glover
   B   Billy Dee Williams   D   Morgan Freeman

18. In *The Blob*, the yucky slime that oozed its way into the hearts of countless horror addicts _____.

    A   emerged from under a rock
    B   was found in an abandoned uranium mine
    C   was developed in a high school science lab
    D   arrived from outer space

19. In *Critters 2*, the poor people of _____ discover that the horrible Krite eggs are producing a new crop of monsters.

    A   Grover's Bend   C   White Plains
    B   Benton Corners   D   Carlton Junction

20. In the frightening feature *Little Monsters*, a young boy encounters a seemingly friendly creature _____.

    A   in a gift-wrapped package
    B   under his bed
    C   in his toy chest
    D   in his kindergarten class

12. Midnight Madness

1. Monkeys are generally pleasant pets, except for the cute little creature in *Monkey Shines* who caused some monstrous monkey business with a _____.

   A   razor   C   knife
   B   gun   D   needle

2. _____ takes place in a remote laboratory in Brazil in which killer insects are developed to be turned loose in the United States.

   A   *Mosquitoes*   C   *The Fly III*
   B   *The Bees*   D   *Killer Bats*

3. In *Christine*, a film of occult overdrive and motorized mayhem, the evil automobile with the supernatural steering was a

   _____.

   A   1964 Escort   C   1958 Plymouth Fury
   B   1962 Oldsmobile Cutlass   D   1974 Corvette

4. In *Silver Bullet*, based upon a novelette by Stephen King, the evil entities terrorizing a small mountain town are opposed by

   _____.

   A   a psychic young girl   C   a feeble old maid
   B   a blind detective   D   a crippled boy

5. At the end of *Child's Play*, cute little Chucky, the murderous doll, was _____.

    A   blown apart by a bomb
    B   chopped up in a giant blender
    C   electrocuted by a monster boom box
    D   crushed and beheaded

6. Oh, that sweet, understanding baby-sitter! She turned out to be a hell of a kid in _____.

    A   *Firestarter*   C   *The Guardian*
    B   *The Believers*   D   *Family Fiend*

7. A teacher of a course in the appreciation of old horror films is the main character in _____.

    A   *Misery*   C   *Ghoulies II*
    B   *Green Card*   D   *Popcorn*

8. In *Tremors*, a gigantic underground monster causes some horrible rumbling and terrifies the residents of a small _____ town.

    A   Nevada   C   Alaska
    B   Florida   D   Hawaii

9. A seven million-year-old object—oozing a strange liquid—is investigated by some science students in _____.

    A   *The Unholy*   C   *Re-Animator*
    B   *Prince of Darkness*   D   *Transmutations*

10. In *Nightlife*, a beautiful vampire awakes after a hundred years and causes some exotic and psychotic problems for a young _____.

    A   lawyer   C   astronaut
    B   rock star   D   doctor

11. *The Abyss*, a nautical nightmare involving deep sea demons, begins with the sinking of a _____.

    A   Japanese fishing boat
    B   private yacht
    C   luxury cruise ship
    D   Navy ship

12. Some hot nuclear waste is guzzled by some six-pack-toting characters (YUCK!) and changes them into blood-seeking demons in

_____.

    A   *Revenge of the Bikers*   C   *Redneck Zombies*
    B   *April Ghouls*   D   *Hitchhikers from Hell*

13. In *The Phantasm: Part Two*, a villainous character known as _____ once more uses his weird assortment of flying daggers to cut some gory capers.

    A   The Tall Man   C   The Dark Man
    B   The Knifeman   D   The Ghost Man

14. Some college students receive an invitation to a hotel they had visited years before only to find that much has changed for the worse in _____.

    A   *Group Death*   C   *Trapped*
    B   *Iced*   D   *Hotel Hell*

15. *The Fantasist*, a slick combination of romance and horror, begins with _____ and ends with a monstrous attack upon an unsuspecting young lady.

    A   a chance meeting on a train
    B   a conversation on a supermarket checkout line
    C   a phone call
    D   a postcard received in the mail

16. A teenage Damien, the delightful devil of the *Omen II*, does his dastardly doings _____.

    A   in a Madison Avenue advertising agency
    B   on a secluded island
    C   in a military academy
    D   in a finishing school for young girls

17. In *It's Alive!*, a newborn demon infant possesses some remarkable _____.

    A   X-ray eyes   C   razor teeth
    B   hairy palms   D   poisoned fingernails

18. In *The Amityville Curse*, the ghost of a murdered _____ is suspected of being the cause of trouble to the occupants of the famous horror house.

    A   actress   C   policeman
    B   priest   D   real estate developer

19. In *Poltergeist III*, poor Carol Ann, in order to escape the evil spirits, moves to _____.

    A   Chicago   C   Miami
    B   Hollywood   D   Las Vegas

20. Oops! *The Slumber Party* has been interrupted by a strange fellow with _____.

    A   an electrified baseball bat
    B   a giant microwave
    C   a portable drill
    D   a bloody electric fan

13. Prowlers & Howlers

1. Robert Englund, the portrayer of Freddy, Elm Street's favorite ghoul, directed the horror film _____.

   A   *976-Evil*   C   *The Unnamable*

   B   *The Newlydeads*   D   *Wolfen*

2. Which of the following major Hollywood stars did *not* appear in one of the *Exorcist* films?

   A   Richard Burton   C   Sean Connery

   B   George C. Scott   D   James Earl Jones

3. In *April Fool's Day*, a captivating coed named _____ invites her college classmates to a deserted island to spend a holiday—which becomes a horror day!

   A   Muffy St. John   C   Tootsie MacDowell

   B   Mitzi Malloy   D   Marla MacDonald

4. Early in his career, Francis Ford Coppola, director of *The Godfather*, directed the low budget bucket-o'-blood about an ax-wielding murderer called _____.

   A   *Asylum 12*   C   *Psycho II*

   B   *Dementia 13*   D   *Madman 4*

5. In *The Texas Chainsaw Massacre 2*, the chain-saw-toting killer is named _____.

    A   Battery Bart   C   Bloodlips
    B   Leatherface   D   Shockface

6. Cockroaches are bad enough, but when they develop a taste for human blood, look out! Of course, this creepy crawling film is named _____.

    A   *The Bugs*   C   *Termites of Terror*
    B   *The Nest*   D   *The Swarm*

7. In *The House II*, a young man decides to dig up the grave of _____ in order to get a skull full of jewels.

    A   an ancient mummy
    B   his great-great-grandfather
    C   Captain Kidd
    D   an electrocuted mass murderer

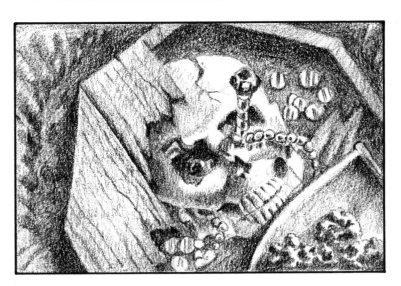

8. Which of the following is *not* the setting of a *Howling* film?

    A   California   C   Transylvania
    B   Australia   D   Hawaii

9. _____ is a witty film that deals with satanic messages in rock music.

A *Full Volume*   C *Trick or Treat*
B *Black Out*   D *Devil's Beat*

10. In the classic British horror film *Dead of Night*, Michael Redgrave played the role of a character dominated by a demonic _____.

A ancient statue   C image in the mirror
B ventriloquist's dummy   D revived mummy

11. Robocop, everybody's favorite super cyborg, did his human and mechanical best to clean up the city of _____.

A Chicago   C New Orleans
B Detroit   D New York

12. In *Robocop 2*, everybody's favorite metallic monster uses his mechanical skills to combat a dangerous new drug called _____.

A Boff   C Pow
B Zap   D Nuke

13. In *The Evil Dead*, in addition to the usual assortment of zombies and demonic possessions, there are some unusual _____ that chill, thrill—and kill.

A trees   C scarecrows
B roses   D fence posts

14. In *Blackbeard's Ghost*, the ghost of the famous pirate shows up in a New England town and gets a job as _____.

A a supermarket manager   C a TV repairman
B a sheriff's deputy   D a college track coach

15. Most of the action of *Dangerous Game*, a flick in which some kids are pursued by a monstrous killer, takes place in a deserted _____.

    A old mansion   C coal mine
    B department store   D western town

16. That masterpiece of yuck, *Son of Blob*, featured _____, one of TV's most popular actors.

    A Larry Hagman   C Don Johnson
    B John Forsythe   D Telly Savalas

17. Poor Police Chief _____! Those Jaws are always out there to munch the summer visitors to his horror-filled seaside town.

    A Brody   C Brennan
    B Barton   D Baker

18. In *The House*, a _____ is almost driven mad by a cute little cottage that seems to possess a demonic spirit.

    A brilliant composer C young bride
    B hardworking writer D talented painter

19. Most *Friday the Thirteenth* fans know everything about the cute little killer Jason except his last name, which is _____.

    A Benton   C Wilder
    B Kruger   D Voorhees

20. _____ played the woman in *Ghostbusters II* who assisted the boys in combatting a slimy mess in the sewers of New York.

    A Julia Roberts   C Sigourney Weaver
    B Meg Ryan   D Madonna

14. TV Terror

1. In *Beauty and the Beast*, Vincent, the gentle beast, lives under the
   city of New York with his _____.

A	father	C	devoted friend, Sam
B	two brothers	D	blind mother

2. Among the most memorable villains opposed by Dr. Who were the
   robot-like creatures called _____.

A	Pertwees	C	Zoabs
B	Daleks	D	Tardons

3. In the TV series *Dracula: The Series*, Dracula is known as Mr.
   _____.

A	Lucard	C	Lugosi
B	Capeman	D	Van Pirson

4. Which of the following was *not* a character in the popular TV series
   Max Headroom?

A	Edison Carter	C	Blank Reg
B	Theora Jones	D	Payson White

5. In *Quantum Leap*, the central figure who can go back through time to relive history is named _____.

    A   Tod Russell   C   Sam Becket

    B   Ken Stewart   D   Joe Holden

6. Much of the action in the TV program *Friday the Thirteenth: The Series* revolves around some _____.

    A   unusual pets owned by a hermit

    B   antique art objects

    C   psychedelic paintings

    D   books of forbidden knowledge

7. *"My Favorite Martian"* lived with a young couple in Los Angeles and was known by the name of _____.

    A   Captain Morton   C   Doctor Marvin

    B   Cousin Crater   D   Uncle Martin

8. The alien Mork left the planet Ork to come to earth, meet Mindy, and have some audience-pleasing adventures in _____.

    A   Fresno, California   C   Boulder, Colorado

    B   Cincinnati, Ohio   D   Santa Fe, New Mexico

9. _____ was the name of the intelligent and mischievous Volkswagen known as the *Love Bug*.

    A   Herbie   C   Billy

    B   Marvin   D   Arthur

10. The Munsters' gloomy mansion was located on _____.

    A   Mockingbird Heights   C   Murky Waters Lane

    B   Coffin Canyon Road   D   Shadow Hill

11. The only normal member of the Munster family was
_____.

    A   Fester   C   Dadwalader
    B   Marilyn   D   Gwen

12. The mother of the witch, Samantha, on the TV series, *Bewitched*, was named _____.

    A   Carlotta   C   Wanda
    B   Morgana   D   Endora

13. The name of the butler on *The Addams Family* was
_____.

    A   Hump   C   Stump
    B   Lurch   D   Crawl

14. Which one of the following was not the name of a character in *The Addams Family* TV series?

    A   Morticia   C   Uncle Fester
    B   Trueheart   D   Gomez

15. A soap opera about a romantic vampire was called
_____.

    A   *Dark Shadows*   C   *Dangerous Waters*
    B   *Journey Into Fear*   D   *Mansions of Mystery*

16. In the TV series *I Dream of Jeannie*, the beautiful genie was married to a young _____.

    A   Hollywood producer   C   press agent
    B   astronaut   D   doctor

17. *The Night That Panicked America* was a made-for-TV movie about an invasion from _____.

    A   Venus   C   Jupiter

    B   a distant galaxy   D   Mars

18. Perry White, Superman's editor, often exclaimed, "Great Caesar's _____!"

    A   ghost   C   lift

    B   spirit   D   shadow

19. A gentleman was transformed into a monstrous giant in _____.

    A   *The Incredible Hulk*   C   *The Man from UNCLE*

    B   *My Favorite Martian*   D   *The Prisoner*

20. The main character in the mystery TV series *The Prisoner* was named _____.

    A   Number 6   C   X-28

    B   Zero   D   Double X

15. Blood & Thud

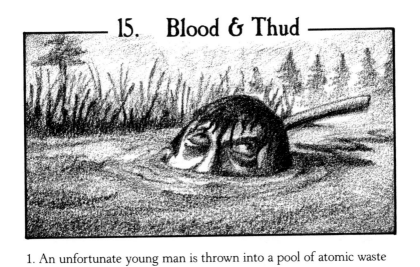

1. An unfortunate young man is thrown into a pool of atomic waste and emerges as a mutant hero in _____.

   A *Alien Ahoy*   C *The Toxic Avenger*
   B *Swamp Thing*   D *Hero of Horror*

2. In *The Intruder*, a crazed killer does a final checkout on some customers as he raises some technicolor hell in a neighborhood _____.

   A pizza shop   C fast food store
   B ice cream parlor   D supermarket

3. In *Psycho II*, Norman Bates returns to his quaint Hitchcock horror motel after serving _____ years in prison.

   A 30   C 15
   B 8   D 22

4. In _____, a young boy adopts a lost golden retriever as his pet and discovers that his cute little doggie may be responsible for a series of gory murders.

   A *The Unearthly*   C *The Toxic Avengers*
   B *The Watchers*   D *The Unnamable*

5. In *Scarecrows*, some diabolical scarecrows leave their curious cornfield to stalk a group of _____.

    A   Boy Scouts   C   weekend campers

    B   circus performers   D   army deserters

6. In *Wolfen*, _____ played the part of the fearless detective who tracked down the vicious animals that attacked a terrified metropolis.

    A   George C. Scott   C   Tom Hanks

    B   Al Pacino   D   Albert Finney

7. The poor _____ family! Wherever they go they seem to be followed, in film after film, by the family poltergeist.

    A   Reynolds   C   Freeling

    B   Williams   D   Lester

8. In *Hellbound: Hellraiser II*, a group of gory cenobites emerges from the Gates of Hell led by one of the cutest of movie monsters, _____.

    A   Red Eyes   C   Jason

    B   Pinhead   D   Firelips

9. In _____, some wild bikers who have weird fun all night and sleep all day turn out to be—you guessed it—vampires!

    A   *Death Race*   C   *Night Monsters*

    B   *Dead Ringers*   D   *The Lost Boys*

10. The ghosts of two young people return to a Connecticut farmhouse to protect it from eccentric interior decorators in the New England frightmare film _____.

    A   *Nightmare*   C   *The Fifth Floor*

    B   *Not of This Earth*   D   *Beetlejuice*

11. In *The Return of the Living Dead,* _____ accidentally release the good old zombies to do some more of their brain munching.

    A   employees of a medical supply company
    B   an absentminded scientist and his beautiful daughter
    C   residents of a rundown nursing home
    D   kids in a junior high school science class

12. A newly married couple is haunted by the spirit of the wife's ex-sweetheart—and the groom's dead(?) brother—in _____.

    A   *Retribution*   C   *Motel Hell*
    B   *Hellraiser*   D   *The Howling II*

13. In *Rabid Grannies,* two grey-haired ladies after _____ turn into senior citizen sadists.

    A   receiving a gift from a relative
    B   being evicted from their cozy home
    C   drinking a potion put in their teacups
    D   attending a strange quilting session

14. In *American Gothic*, Ma and Pa, the heads of a demented family that enjoys killing unsuspecting visitors to their remote island, were played by _____.

    A   Rod Steiger and Cloris Leachman
    B   Paul Newman and Joanne Woodward
    C   Vincent Price and Jean Stapleton
    D   Richard Burton and Elizabeth Taylor

15. Under the green moss of the ugly *Swamp Thing* beats the kind heart of _____, avenger of evil.

    A   Captain William White   C   Professor Thomas Drew
    B   Dr. Alec Holland   D   Father Patrick Doyle

16. In a classic horror film, an enterprising scientist decides to test his newly developed invention on himself, but—oops—a _____ gets in the way and is transformed into a gigantic monster.

    A   fly   C   bee
    B   caterpillar   D   mouse

17. *Fright Night* begins when a teenage boy starts to suspect that his _____ is a vampire.

    A   high school football coach
    B   school guidance counselor
    C   next door neighbor
    D   sister's boy friend

18. *The Lair of the* _____ by Bram Stoker, author of *Dracula*, tells the gruesome tale of a young man who must be sacrificed in order to restore an ancient monster to life.

    A   *Green Goddess*   C   *Egyptian Cat*
    B   *White Worm*   D   *Devil Bat*

19. In *Monkey Shines: An Experiment in Fear*, a young man, confined to a wheelchair, is aided by a super-intelligent monkey named _____.

    A   Marlene   C   Maralyn
    B   Greta   D   Ella

20. The film *Something Wicked This Way Comes*, based on the famous story by Ray Bradbury, tells of the weird doings in _____.

    A   Professor Pine's Traveling Troupe
    B   Count Dracula's Drama Society
    C   Dr. Death's Gothic Ensemble
    D   Mr. Dark's Pandemonium Carnival

16.   Splatter & Shatter

1. *Cujo* was the name of a cuddly St. Bernard who changed into a monstrous killer after being bitten by a _____.

    A   fly   C   rat
    B   bat   D   wolf

2. Even experts on *The Rocky Horror Show* may have trouble naming the young actor and actress who played the part of the couple stranded in the weirdo castle. They were _____.

    A   Jessica Lange and Michael Keaton
    B   Susan Sarandon and Barry Bostwick
    C   Farrah Fawcett and Kevin Costner
    D   Kim Basinger and Tom Cruise

3. In *Frankenhooker*, a young lady is killed by—would you believe it?—_____.

    A   a runaway lawn mower
    B   a demon snowblower
    C   a gas-spraying vacuum cleaner
    D   a demonic VCR

4. In *Satan's* _____, an ex-cop, searching for a missing girl, runs into some occult occurrences involving a beautiful monster.

A   *Mistress*   C   *Princess*
B   *Sister*   D   *Siren*

5. In *Return to Horror High*, former pupils and teachers of Crippen High are reunited through the efforts of _____.

A   a professional reunion service
B   a motion picture company
C   a team of atomic scientists
D   a group of friendly aliens

6. A revengeful father in the film _____ enlists the aid of a witch and her gang of graveyard ghouls to punish the killers of his son.

A   *Pumpkinhead*   C   *Rituals*
B   *Intruder*   D   *Twice Dead*

7. You might enjoy a movie intermission at your favorite candy stand, but not when the concession is run by the psychotic popcorn pusher in _____.

A   *The Anguish*   C   *The Dead*
B   *The Cage*   D   *The Mommy*

8. Satan's Den, a ramshackle fun house at a rundown amusement park, is the setting of some unfunny doings in _____.

A   *Schizo 5*   C   *Boogeyman 4*
B   *Ghoulies II*   D   *The Howling 3*

9. In Stephen King's *Misery*, the unfortunate character who is tortured by a monstrously misguided fan is a noted _____.

A   novelist   C   rock star
B   movie star   D   TV anchorman

10. In the grippingly gruesome film _____, an American family moves to Sweden and discovers there is a strange presence in their attic.

   A   *The Visitors*   C   *Northern Lights*
   B   *Nightmare House*   D   *A Stranger Is Watching*

11. In _____, a demonic spirit is revived by some young girls holding a seance in a funeral parlor.

   A   *Halloween Four*   C   *Demon's Return*
   B   *Night of the Demons*   D   *They're Alive*

12. All sorts of electrical appliances gang up to form a horrible team of AC-DC monsters in _____.

   A   *The House*   C   *Live Wires*
   B   *Pulse*   D   *Project X*

13. In *The Berserkers*, a re-animated monster with the head of a wolf shows up in a peaceful _____ town.

   A   Canadian   C   Wisconsin
   B   Rhode Island   D   Texas

14. George Romero and Stephen King teamed up to produce the macabre masterpiece _____.

   A   *The Thing*   C   *The Amityville Horror*
   B   *Firestarter*   D   *Creepshow*

15. A trio of nasty ten-year-old kids goes on a killing spree in which they eliminate neighbors, relatives and other helpless characters, in

_____.

   A   *Something Wild*   C   *Bloody Birthday*
   B   *Red Dawn*   D   *The Chase*

16. Stephen King made his debut as a film director in _____.

    A   *Carrie*   C   *Maximum Overdrive*

    B   *The Shining*   D   *Pet Sematary*

17. The first *Halloween* film tells the gruesome story of a maniac who returns to a small town where, fifteen years before, he had murdered _____.

    A   his father   C   his entire family

    B   his best friend   D   his sister

18. In *Fright Night*, Roddy MacDowell, a has-been show host, subjects _____ to an unusual vampire test.

    A   Robert Loggia   C   Sandy Dennis

    B   Chris Sarandon   D   Tony Lo Bianco

19. The setting of many of the creepy blood-curdling capers in the *Friday the Thirteenth* fright film is _____.

    A   Elm City Shopping Mall   C   Camp Crystal Lake

    B   Morstan Mansion   D   Mason City

20. In *Friday the 13th: Part VI Jason Lives*, director Tom McLoughlin pays tribute to a horror great of yore by having Jason pass _____.

    A   Karloff's General Store

    B   Lugosi's Lounge

    C   Chaney's Ice-cream Parlor

    D   Vincent Price Videos

17. Muck & Yuck

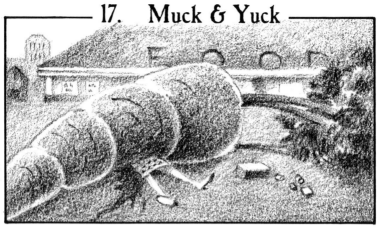

1. An attack by a group of monstrous carrots was the juicy subject of
_____.

    A *Invasion of the Saucer Man*
    B *Attack of the Killer Plants*
    C *Day of the Triffids*
    D *Green Slime*

2. In _____, an army of beautiful aliens and an ugly clump
of seaweed slipped into earth for some deadly doings.

    A *Invasion of the Star Creatures*
    B *Invasion of the Puppet People*
    C *Queen of Death*
    D *Rock All Night*

3. In *The Invasion of the Body-Snatchers* (1956), the distinguished
director _____ appeared in a bit part as a meter reader.

    A George Romero   C George Lucas
    B Sam Peckinpaugh   D Ken Russell

4. A 14-year-old girl was possessed by a mysterious power in
_____.

    A *The Omen*   C *The Fog*
    B *The Sentinel*   D *The Exorcist*

5. A group of tentacled vegetarian creatures from outer space grabbed, groped and grappled in _____.

    A   *The Navy vs. the Night Monster*
    B   *Them!*
    C   *The Purple Monsters Strike*
    D   *Terrornauta*

6. A kindly alien from outer space came to earth to order a halt in the production of atomic energy in _____.

    A   *THX-1138*
    B   *Time Travelers*
    C   *Twenty Million Miles to Earth*
    D   *The Day the Earth Stood Still*

7. Morlocks, the ape-like creatures who lived under the earth, had some dark secrets in _____.

    A   *Visit to a Small Planet*   C   *Target Earth*
    B   *The Time Machine*   D   *Slaughterhouse Five*

8. The name of the robot who assumed command of the spaceship in *2001: A Space Odyssey* was _____.

    A   Bob   C   Mac
    B   Tob   D   Hal

9. *Attack of the Fifty Foot* _____ may be one of the weirdest films ever made.

    A   *Aunt*   C   *Spider*
    B   *Monster*   D   *Woman*

10. The Creature from the Black Lagoon was first found _____.

    A   on a hill in Africa   C   in a Louisiana swamp
    B   in the Amazon jungle   D   on Skull island

11. In _____, an alien spacecraft was manned by a crew of
giant skeletons as it raced through the solar system.

    A   *Voyage to the Prehistoric Planet*
    B   *Planet on the Prowl*
    C   *Planet of the Vampires*
    D   *They Came from Beyond Space*

12. The opening scene of the movie classic _____ showed a
pretty girl being pursued by a corpse in a deserted cemetery.

    A   *Mad Monster Party*
    B   *Nightmare in Wax*
    C   *It Conquered the World*
    D   *Night of the Living Dead*

13. A Martian princess and her drooling assistant sent an army of
aliens to conquer earth in _____.

    A   *Aliens of Blood*
    B   *They Came From Planet X*
    C   *Frankenstein Meets the Space Monster*
    D   *Space Killers*

14. In _____ a strange alien—half man, half machine—fell in love with a scientist's beautiful daughter.

    A   *Moon Zero Two*   C   *Destination Inner Space*
    B   *Mission Stardust*   D   *Cyborg 2087*

15. Talos, a bronze warrior, was brought to life in _____.

    A   *Godzilla vs. The Thing*
    B   *Konga*
    C   *Reptilucus*
    D   *Jason and the Argonauts*

16. In _____, a heavenly messenger showed a young man what his hometown could have been like if he had never been born.

    A   *When We Live Again*   C   *It's a Wonderful Life*
    B   *Sad Yesterday*   D   *Mad Wednesday*

17. Name the picture that was so shocking—or so bad—that it used a "fear flasher," in order to warn the audience not to look at its most horrible scenes.

    A   *Tron*   C   *Chamber of Horrors*
    B   *Flesh*   D   *The Atomic Brain*

18. A honeymoon couple, stranded in a ruined castle, encountered an entire gallery of horrible characters in _____.

    A   *The Rocky Horror Show*   C   *House of Hate*
    B   *Castle Skull*   D   *The Strange Door*

19. A wealthy suburban community was inhabited by almost "perfect" women who were mysteriously dominated by their husbands in

_____.

    A   *You'll Like My Mother*   C   *The Stepford Wives*
    B   *Man Made Monsters*   D   *Hurry Sundown*

20. One remarkable feature of the children in *Village of the Damned* was their:

    A   extraordinary eyes
    B   their ability to walk through walls
    C   their acute sense of hearing
    D   their ability to communicate with animals

IV
FACT, FOLKLORE
& FICTION

18. Monsters in Mythology

1. Another name for the Abominable Snowman of the Himalayan Mountains is _____.

   A   Sarak   C   Yeti
   B   Tiki   D   Ralina

2. _____ was a small mythical horse with one horn.

   A   An orphion   C   A griffin
   B   An oread   D   A unicorn

3. _____ are horrible little creatures who are believed to inhabit the woods of Scandinavia.

   A   Lamias   C   Banshees
   B   Trolls   D   Orcs

4. _____ are invisible creatures that are believed to hurl objects around rooms.

   A   Hesperides   C   Gremlins
   B   Poltergeists   D   Espograms

5. The _____ is believed to be an eternal bird of life with the power to rise from its own ashes.

   A   phoenix   C   helix
   B   sphinx   D   asperata

6. _____ was a legendary winged horse who was tamed by Bellerophon.

   A   Tauraus   C   Hydra
   B   Cerebrus   D   Pegasus

7. _____ was the goat-legged son of Hermes who protected shepherds' flocks.

   A   Oberon   C   Loki
   B   Pan   D   Narcissus

8. _____, a Babylonian god with a large stomach, loved to devour children.

   A   Baal   C   Ra
   B   Moloch   D   Azalzec

9. The legendary _____ were half women, half fish.

   A   mermaids   C   Amazons
   B   Hesperides   D   Draconians

10. The _____ were fierce Greek women who often devoured people when carried away by religious frenzy.

   A   Syrinxes   C   Nimrods
   B   Maenads   D   Gorgons

11. Queen _____ is a tiny fairy queen whose little chariot is drawn by flying ants.

   A   Toth   C   Titania
   B   Mab   D   Thalia

12. The Greek hero Hercules killed _____, a nine-headed serpent.

    A Lothar   C Polyphemus
    B Hydra   D Patrocles

13. _____ were ugly stone figures placed on the top of buildings in the Middle Ages to frighten off evil spirits.

    A Sirens   C Lamias
    B Gargoyles   D Titans

14. In Egyptian mythology, the god Osiris had the head of a _____.

    A lion   C goat
    B fish   D jackal

15. The English hero Beowulf killed _____, a terrible monster.

    A Gopus   C Fafner
    B Grendel   D Osric

16. _____ was a snake-haired she-monster whose looks turned men to stone.

    A A merrow   C A gorgon
    B A harpy   D An incubus

17. _____, a legendary Greek sorceress, turned men into swine.

    A Urania   C Euterpe
    B Clio   D Circe

18. In Teutonic mythology, _____ was a giant who transformed himself into a dragon.

    A Wotan   C Loki
    B Fafner   D Fritga

19. Arabian spirits called _____ are believed to whirl around the desert as dark clouds.

    A rukhs   C myung-kim
    B djinns   D alaphs

20. _____ was the cat-headed Egyptian goddess of fire.

    A Bast   C Gard-Re
    B Tor   D Carib

19. Werewolves & Vampires

1. The word "werewolf" means _____.

    A   man wolf   C   half wolf

    B   night wolf   D   part wolf

2. A classic story by the ancient Roman writer Petronius tells how _____ transformed himself into a wolf.

    A   an emperor   C   a soldier

    B   a slave   D   a beggar

3. Ancient Roman legends relate the story of a she-wolf who suckled twins named _____.

    A   Castor and Pollux   C   Ares and Apollo

    B   David and Jonathan   D   Romulus and Remus

4. The belief in vampires became widespread in Europe after the _____ epidemic in 1347.

    A   smallpox   C   cholera

    B   Red Death   D   Black Death

5. A _____ was needed to kill a werewolf, according to the folk legends of Scotland.

    A broken jar   C wooden shoe
    B silver bullet   D hound's tooth

6. In _____ it was believed that werewolves hung their skins on nearby trees at their yearly meetings.

    A North America   C Alaska
    B Serbia   D Finland

7. According to Greek mythology, the evil _____ was transformed into a werewolf by Zeus.

    A King Midas   C Queen Clytemnestra
    B Prince Lycaon   D Cyclops

8. According to Christian legend, _____ changed a cruel king into a wolf.

    A St. Elmo   C St. George
    B St. Francis   D St. Patrick

9. Real vampire bats exist in _____.

    A   the mountains of Transylvania
    B   the Fiji Islands
    C   South Africa
    D   the jungles of South America

10. Which statement about belief in the existence of vampires is true?

    A   Many primitive societies all over the world believed in vampires.
    B   Only the peasants of Transylvania believed in vampires.
    C   Vampires were believed to exist only in Europe.
    D   The Chinese do not believe in vampires.

11. A belief in werewolves may have been originated from the fact that ancient Norse warriors, known as _____, wore wolfskins or bearskins in battle.

    A   Norskers   C   Lunares
    B   Berserkers   D   Lokis

12. In ancient times, it was believed that a person who ate the flesh of a _____ killed by a wolf might become a werewolf.

    A   child   C   cow
    B   sheep   D   pig

13. "The Witches' Kitchen," a famous painting by _____, shows people being transformed into wolf-like creatures.

    A   Velazquez   C   Titian
    B   Goya   D   El Greco

14. _____, the great explorer, described people with the heads of dogs.

    A   Christopher Columbus   C   Vasco da Gama
    B   Marco Polo   D   Henry Hudson

15. In ancient times, _____ was known as "wolf land."

   A   Ireland   C   Sweden
   B   Spain   D   Finland

16. According to Avicenna, one of the most distinguished physicians of the Middle Ages, wolf mania is most common during the month of _____.

   A   February   C   July
   B   September   D   August

17. The trial of _____, perhaps the most renowned vampire trial in French history, took place in 1849.

   A   Sergeant Bertrand C   General Ludoc
   B   Captain Picard   D   Dr. Fremont

18. According to Scandinavian folklore, the belt of a werewolf must have _____ notches.

   A   three   C   ten
   B   seven   D   two

19. A popular Russian folktale tells of the adventures of _____ and the Wolf.

   A   Ivan   C   Peter
   B   Igor   D   Anton

20. In France, a werewolf is called a _____.

   A   loup garou   C   loup de nuit
   B   loup morte   D   loup sauvage

20. Mysterious Mummies

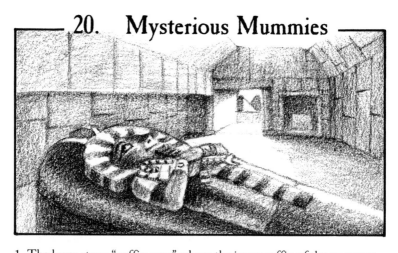

1. The large stone "coffin case" where the inner coffin of the mummy was placed is called a _____.

   A   thoraxa
   B   mastaba
   C   genatrix
   D   sarcophagus

2. Before the building of the great pyramids, royal mummies were often buried in tombs called _____.

   A   karas
   B   mastabas
   C   luxoras
   D   sphinxes

3. Egyptians who couldn't afford to be buried as mummies were often buried _____.

   A   in mountain caves
   B   in special burial buildings set aside for the poor
   C   in large clay vases
   D   in the desert sand

4. The name of each mummy was most often written on the _____.

   A   mummy's outer coffin
   B   linen bindings
   C   lid of the sarcophagus
   D   wall of the tomb

5. The one organ that was usually left in place within the body of the mummy was the _____.

    A   lungs   C   small intestine
    B   liver   D   heart

6. Egyptian mummies were often transported to their tombs _____.

    A   in a golden chariot
    B   on a sled pulled by oxen
    C   on the shoulders of three men
    D   on a special three-wheeled cart

7. The portrait masks of many mummies often included a braided beard, symbolic of the god _____.

    A   Osiris   C   Theta
    B   Isis   D   Zeus

8. Each corpse was _____ to allow fluids and moisture to leave the body before mummification.

    A   placed out in the sun for seven days
    B   placed high on a hilltop for thirteen days
    C   placed on an inclined embalming board
    D   buried in the sand and dug up in nine days

9. The writings on the walls of many ancient Egyptian tombs are called _____.

    A   sanskrits   C   coptics
    B   hieroglyphics   D   aramaics

10. In most cases, embalmers wrapped the mummy in _____ layers of linen.

    A   ten   C   six
    B   twenty   D   seven

11. When the heart was removed from the body of the mummy, it was replaced with a _____.

    A   stone image of a heart
    B   stone scarab
    C   large jewel
    D   wreath of consecrated flowers

12. If a royal mummy was transported to his tomb by boat, the boat was _____.

    A   broken into smaller pieces and buried in the tomb
    B   buried near the tomb
    C   sunk by a priest in the River Nile
    D   blessed by a priest and returned to the royal palace

13. The mummy's nostrils were stuffed with _____.

    A   beeswax
    B   clay
    C   a special ointment containing crushed flowers
    D   precious jewels

14. The tomb of King Tut was discovered in _____.

   A   1910   C   1948
   B   1922   D   1894

15. The tomb of King Tut was found_____.

   A   in the Aswan region
   B   in the Valley of the Kings
   C   on the outskirts of Cairo
   D   near the pyramids of Gizah

16. King Tut was _____ years old when he died.

   A   88   C   24
   B   17   D   62

17. The inner coffin where the mummy of King Tut was found was made of _____.

   A   solid gold   C   brass
   B   cedar with inlaid jewels   D   iron

18. The legend of the curse of King Tut may have started because Lord Carnarvon, the man who financed the discovery of Tut's tomb, died _____ after the great discovery.

   A   ten days   C   two days
   B   one month   D   five months

19. The archeologist who first entered King Tut's tomb died _____ after his great discovery.

   A   one week   C   one month
   B   18 years   D   exactly seven years

20. The tomb of King Tut consisted of a corridor, a treasury room and _____ chambers.

   A   ten   C   six
   B   three   D   four

21. Witchery in History

1. A group of witches is called a _____.

    A   coven   C   school

    B   pact   D   carol

2. When a group of witches gathered in the woods to practice their mysterious rites, they were said to be indulging in a _____.

    A   spell circle   C   convocation

    B   devilry   D   Sabbat

3. A cat, dog or any small animal that accompanied a witch was known as the witch's _____.

    A   Lucifer   C   goblin

    B   spirit   D   familiar

4. At witchcraft trials, the accused were often tested by the odd method of _____.

    A   being forced to drink gallons of red wine

    B   being locked in a pigsty

    C   being fed hot muffins

    D   being dunked in water

5. The Old Testament relates the story of _____, who consulted the Witch of Endor.

   A Joshua   C Saul
   B David   D Solomon

6. One of the traditional rituals of dealing with suspected witches was a strange ceremony involving a bell, book and _____.

   A cross   C bible
   B broom   D candle

7. In 1633 Urbain Grandier, a priest, was tried and burned at the stake for having bewitched a number of nuns at their convent in _____.

   A Marseilles   C Calais
   B St. Michel   D Loudun

8. The first outbreak of suspected witchcraft in Salem, Massachusetts, which eventually led to the infamous witchcraft trials, occurred in the home of _____.

   A Reverend George Burroughs
   B Reverend John Hale
   C Reverend John Dalton
   D Reverend Samuel Parris

9. _____, known as the "modern Merlin," practiced his black arts at the court of Queen Elizabeth I.

   A Dr. Gabriel Lopez   C Dr. John Dee
   B Roger Bacon   D Judge Samuel Coke

10. King _____ of Scotland personally interrogated suspected witches at a trial in North Berwick in 1590.

   A Charles   C James
   B Richard   D John

11. In 1593, the landmark British witchcraft trial of the
_____ established the "validity" of children being able to
bewitch their elders.

    A   Chelmsford Five   C   Burton Boys
    B   Sprague sisters   D   Montieth brothers

12. During the mid-1600's, at the height of the witchcraft mania in
England, _____ was known as the Witch Finder General.

    A   Matthew Hopkins   C   Thomas Tudor
    B   Ezekial White   D   Lord Burleigh

13. The first significant English book to attack witchcraft as a base-
less superstition was *The Discovery of Witchcraft* (1584) by
_____.

    A   Reginald Scot   C   Sir Walter Raleigh
    B   Francis Bacon   D   The Earl of Oxford

14. *The Wonders of the Invisible World* (1693), by the distinguished
Puritan clergyman _____, accepted witchcraft as a horrible reality.

    A   Roger Chillingworth   C   Cotton Mather
    B   John Alden   D   Jonathan Edwards

15. If a defendant "stood mute" by refusing to plead either guilty or
not guilty to the charge of witchcraft, the usual punishment in
New England was _____.

    A   to be imprisoned for twenty years
    B   to be pressed to death
    C   to be stoned to death
    D   to be confined in the stocks until he starved to death

16. The most well known American witchcraft trial took place in Salem, Massachusetts, in _____.

    A   1708   C   1692
    B   1645   D   1623

17. According to popular Christian tradition, the wizard Simon Magus was destroyed when the sign of the cross was made by _____.

    A   the Apostle Peter   C   St. Augustine
    B   St. Patrick   D   Albertus Magnus

18. An ancestor of one of America's most distinguished literary masters, _____, was a judge of the infamous Salem witchcraft trials.

    A   Herman Melville   C   Edgar Allan Poe
    B   Nathaniel Hawthorne   D   Henry James

19. An outstanding American play about witchcraft in New England is entitled _____.

   A   *The Trial*   C   *Blithe Spirit*
   B   *The Crucible*   D   *Seven Keys to Baldpate*

20. One of the great masterpieces of Dutch painting is the portrait of Mallie Babbe, the sorceress of Haarlem, by _____.

   A   Rembrandt   C   Vermeer
   B   Hals   D   Breughel

22. Shudders from Shakespeare

1. Which of Shakespeare's characters spoke the line, "Alas poor ghost"?

   A   Brutus   C   Macbeth
   B   Hamlet   D   Shylock

2. During the Elizabethan period, the stage of a typical theatre had a _____ to accommodate the appearance of a theatrical ghost.

   A   special curtain
   B   trap door
   C   a ladder leading to the roof
   D   overhead pulley

3. Shakespeare's greatest rival, Christopher Marlowe, wrote about a character who made a pact with the devil in his classic drama _____.

   A   *Doctor Faustus*   C   *Edward II*
   B   *Tamburlaine the Great*   D   *The Jew of Malta*

4. Which of the following Shakespearan characters was visited by the ghosts of his murder victims?

   A   Richard II   C   Cassius
   B   Richard III   D   Pericles

5. In *Henry the Sixth, Part I*, Shakespeare portrays Joan of Arc, known as La Pucelle, as a shrewd and merciless witch who _____.

    A   summoned up demons from the underworld
    B   cast a spell upon a queen of England
    C   strangled a newborn babe
    D   blinded an archbishop

6. The only indoor appearance of the ghost of Hamlet's father takes place in _____.

    A   a throne room   C   a dark corridor
    B   a bedchamber   D   a chapel

7. The ghost of Julius Caesar appeared to Brutus on the eve of the battle of _____.

    A   Salamis   C   Philippi
    B   Tuscany   D   Arbela

8. The most universally quoted line uttered by a Shakespearean ghost is _____.

    A   "Alas, poor Yorick"
    B   "Leave her to heaven"
    C   "The play's the thing"
    D   "This above all, to thine own self be true"

9. Which of the following was *not* an ingredient in the infernal concoction that the witches in *Macbeth* brewed to conjure up their ghostly apparitions?

    A   wool of bat   C   beak of a bird
    B   toe of a frog   D   eye of a newt

10. The ghost of Banquo, covered with blood, appeared to Macbeth
_____.

    A   at a banquet   C   on a battlefield
    B   on a foggy moor   D   on a castle wall

11. In *Cymbeline* a soothsayer is called upon in the final scene to foretell the future of _____.

    A   the ruling family of Genoa
    B   an heir to the throne of Scotland
    C   a newly married couple
    D   Britain and Rome

12. Which one of the following Shakespearean characters may be described as a wizard possessing magical powers?

    A   Angelo   C   Coriolanus
    B   Timon   D   Prospero

13. In one of Shakespeare's most popular plays, a number of ghosts appear in the English countryside near _____.

    A   Windsor Castle   C   Bosworth Field
    B   Sherwood Forest   D   Hampton Court

14. Much of the mistaken identity action of *A Midsummer Night's Dream* stems from a quarrel between Oberon, King of the Fairies, and his queen, _____.

    A   Hermia   C   Titania
    B   Helena   D   Thisbe

15. Which one of the following Shakespearean characters may be accurately described as a son of a witch?

    A   Puck   C   Pyramus
    B   Caliban   D   Trinculo

16. A ghost appears in all the following plays except _____.

    A   *Hamlet*   C   *Richard III*

    B   *Macbeth*   D   *Othello*

17. According to theatrical tradition, the role of the ghost in the original production of *Hamlet* was played by _____.

    A   William Shakespeare   C   Richard Burbage

    B   Ben Jonson   D   Philip Henslowe

18. A short scene from *The Witch* by _____ is often interpolated into *Macbeth* in order to add supernatural elements as well as length to Shakespeare's shortest major tragedy.

    A   Ben Jonson   C   John Webster

    B   Christopher Marlowe   D   Thomas Middleton

19. One of Shakespeare's most charming spirits, an inhabitant of an enchanted island, is the ingenious and invisible _____.

    A   Rosalind   C   Ariel

    B   Portia   D   Volumnia

20. Did Shakespeare believe in ghosts when he wrote the immortal line, "There are more things in heaven and earth, _____, than are dreamt of in your philosophy."?

    A   Antony   C   Brutus

    B   Horatio   D   Shylock

23. Frightening Fiction

1. _____ is a classic American short story by Nathaniel Hawthorne in which a scarecrow was brought to life by an old hag.

   A   "The Artist of the Beautiful"
   B   "The Transmigration of a Soul"
   C   "The Ambitious Guest"
   D   "Feathertop"

2. A young governess was terrified by two ghosts who haunted two young children in *The Turn of the Screw* by _____.

   A   Nathaniel Hawthorne   C   Stephen Crane
   B   Jack London   D   Henry James

3. *The Castle of* _____ by Horace Walpole was one of the first successful Gothic novels written in English.

   A   *Horror*   C   *Glom*
   B   *Verono*   D   *Otranto*

4. In Oscar Wilde's *The Picture of* _____, the portrait of an immoral young man underwent a grotesque transformation.

   A   *Tom Jones*   C   *Dorian Gray*
   B   *Joseph Andrews*   D   *Roderick Hudson*

5. A young woman, believed to be dead, was buried prematurely in
_____.

    A   "The Triumph of Night"
    B   "The Fair God"
    C   "Berenice"
    D   "The Fall of the House of Usher"

6. A mysterious house, a gentle spinster and a skeleton are elements
in the celebrated horror tale _____.

    A   "Barn Burning"   C   "The Open Window"
    B   "Noon Wine"   D   "A Rose for Emily"

7. "Moxon's _____", by Ambrose Bierce, was one of the first
stories about a man-made creature in American literature.

    A   Monster   C   Machine
    B   Image   D   Master

8. A young lady was terrified by mysterious spirits in an eerie
mansion in _____ *Abbey* by Jane Austen.

    A   *Castleton*   C   *Buckingham*
    B   *Northanger*   D   *Carfax*

9. The great English novelist _____ wrote the memorable
Letters on Demonology and Witchcraft.

    A   Charles Dickens   C   George Eliot
    B   Sir Walter Scott   D   William Thackeray

10. A savage ape committed horrible murders in Edgar Allan Poe's
_____.

    A   "The Mystery of Marie Roget"
    B   "The Murders in the Rue Morgue"
    C   "The Tell-Tale Heart"
    D   "Bon Bon"

11. "Lamia," a gripping poem about a vampire who lured men to their death, was written by the English romantic poet _____.

    A   Keats   C   Shelley

    B   Wordsworth   D   Byron

12. Charles Dickens' classic tale _____ is an eerie story of a man destroyed by a ghostly spirit.

    A   "The Flower of Science"   C   "Silence"

    B   "The Signalman"   D   "Red Hands"

13. "For the Blood Is the Life" is _____ classic story of a female vampire who came back from the dead to haunt her lover.

    A   Stephen Crane's   C   George Eliot's

    B   Emily Bronte's   D   Marion Crawford's

14. In _____ by Guy de Maupassant, an invisible force possessed a man's mind.

    A   "The Wandering Spirit"   C   "The Coward"

    B   "The Horla"   D   "The Ambassador"

15. "The Red Room" is a masterful tale by _____ about a man who accepted a challenge to spend a night in a haunted room.

   A   H. G. Wells   C   Biona McCleod
   B   Guy de Maupassant   D   Rudyard Kipling

16. A timid and insecure spirit is treated sympathetically in "The _____ Ghost" by Oscar Wilde.

   A   Sussex   C   Chapel
   B   Canterville   D   Cathedral

17. In _____ by Edgar Allan Poe, a deformed court jester burned his master and his friends to death to gain revenge.

   A   "Hop Frog"   C   "Metzengerstein"
   B   "Morella"   D   "Bon Bon"

18. "The Terrible Strange Bed" by _____ is about people who are found dead in a terribly strange bed!

   A   Wilkie Collins   C   Jane Austen
   B   Sir Walter Scott   D   Ann Radcliffe

19. In "The Body Snatcher" by _____, corpses were raised from the grave for scientific purposes.

   A   Charles Dickens   C   Wilkie Collins
   B   Robert Louis Stevenson   D   Henry James

20. For 3,000 years, a beautiful woman awaited the return of her lover in _____ by H. Rider Haggard.

   A   *She*   C   *King Solomon's Mines*
   B   *The Eternal Return*   D   *Sheba*

24. Scary Stories

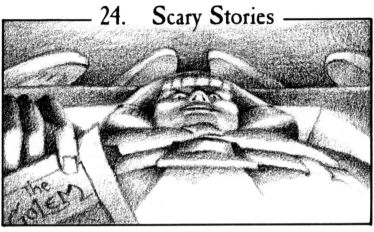

1. The legendary Golem, a man-made monster, was created by
_____.

    A   Doctor Faustus
    B   a wise rabbi
    C   a mad scientist
    D   a disfigured laboratory assistant

2. A gourmet restaurant featured a strange delicacy of human flesh in
"The Specialty of the House" by _____.

    A   John Collier   C   Stanley Ellin
    B   John Cheever   D   H.P. Lovecraft

3. Lestat, the most popular vampire of the 1980s, is the creation of
the brilliant writer of supernatural fiction _____.

    A   Peter Straub   C   Ira Levin
    B   Anne Rice   D   Stephen King

4. Charles Maturin's _____ *the Wanderer* is widely regarded
as one of the great classics of horror and terror.

    A   *Hawley*   C   *Orson*
    B   *Warner*   D   *Melmoth*

5. In *Wieland* by Charles Brockden Brown, one of the earliest American Gothic novels, a diabolical _____ terrified a rural Pennsylvania family.

   A   scientist   C   acrobat
   B   student   D   ventriloquist

6. The werewolf theme appears in the classic American short story, "The German Student" by _____.

   A   Herman Melville   C   Washington Irving
   B   Nathaniel Hawthorne   D   Henry James

7. *The Mysteries of* _____ by Ann Radcliffe, one of the most celebrated novels of the 18th century, is the story of two young lovers who encounter strange experiences in a mysterious castle.

   A   *Oberto*   C   *Oporto*
   B   *Udolpho*   D   *Accosta*

8. A man's struggle with an invisible being is the subject of "What Was It?" by _____.

   A   Nathaniel Hawthorne   C   Brander Matthews
   B   Fitz-James O'Brien   D   Edgar Allan Poe

9. Lord Byron's frightening poem _____ is a tale of a vampire who destroyed his loved ones.

   A   "The Giaour"   C   "A Vision of Judgment"
   B   "Heaven and Hell"   D   "Address to the Devil"

10. Ghostly apparitions and a clutching hand possessed a London house in "The Haunter and the Haunted" by the celebrated English author _____.

   A   Wilkie Collins   C   Charles Dickens
   B   Jane Austen   D   Sir Arthur Conan Doyle

11. An idol came to life to reclaim the priceless jewel stolen from its shrine in *A Night at* _____ by Lord Dunsany.

    A   *the Inn*   C   *the Museum*

    B   *the Castle*   D   *the Abbey*

12. M.R. James' thrilling tale _____ is an eerie story about a child who learned about his vampire ancestry.

    A   "The Royal Game"   C   "Rex"

    B   "The Game of Kings"   D   "Count Magnus"

13. In "The Mark of the Beast" by _____, a man displayed some grotesque animal traits.

    A   Robert Louis Stevenson   C   William Faulkner

    B   Charles Dickens   D   Rudyard Kipling

14. An old woman, a dog, and a horrible act of revenge are the elements in "Vendetta" by the master of the short story _____.

    A   O. Henry   C   H. G. Wells

    B   Guy de Maupassant   D   Anton Chekhov

15. In "Lot No. 249" an Egyptian mummy was brought back to life after thousands of years in an ancient tomb. The author of this grim tale is _____.

    A   Sir Arthur Conan Doyle   C   Victor Hugo

    B   Jules Verne   D   Oscar Wilde

16. "Automatons" is a gripping 18th century story about a robot-like creature by _____.

    A   Voltaire   C   E.T.A. Hoffman

    B   Jonathan Swift   D   Horace Walpole

17. After two centuries, the soul of a dead man rose from the grave to fasten itself upon the flesh of the living in Walter de la Mare's _____.

    A "Welcome Home"   C "A.V. Laider"
    B "The Return"   D "When the Dead Arise"

18. "Mrs. _____," by a master creator of ghostly tales, E.F. Benson, is a memorable story about a female vampire.

    A Page   C Payton
    B Amworth   D Andrews

19. *The King in Yellow*, an unforgettable horror tale by Robert W. Chambers, is about a mysterious _____ that caused people to go mad.

    A statue   C necklace
    B portrait   D book

20. A man becomes a "nearly liquid mass of loathsome, of detestable putrescence" in Edgar Allan Poe's horror classic _____.

    A "William Wilson"
    B "The Facts of the Case of M. Valdemar"
    C "Never Bet the Devil Your Head"
    D "M.S. Found in a Bottle"

ANSWERS

I DRACULA & FRANKENSTEIN

1. Yes, There Was a Dracula

1. B	2. C	3. B	4. D	5. B
6. C	7. D	8. D	9. B	10. B
11. D	12. B	13. B	14. B	15. B
16. C	17. A	18. C	19. A	20. C

2. Transylvania Mania

1. A	2. C	3. D	4. D	5. C
6. A	7. D	8. B	9. D	10. A
11. B	12. B	13. D	14. B	15. D
16. B	17. C	18. B	19. D	20. B

3. Draculas by the Dozen

1. A	2. B	3. B	4. A	5. A
6. A	7. C	8. A	9. D	10. B
11. C	12. D	13. B	14. D	15. C
16. B	17. D	18. D	19. D	20. B

4. Frankenstein: the Novel

1. B	2. A	3. A	4. B	5. B
6. B	7. B	8. A	9. B	10. D
11. B	12. A	13. B	14. B	15. B
16. D	17. B	18. B	19. B	20. A

5. Frankenstein: the Films

1. A	2. A	3. C	4. A	5. A
6. B	7. A	8. B	9. B	10. C
11. D	12. D	13. C	14. D	15. D
16. A	17. D	18. B	19. B	20. B

II CLASSIC MOVIE MONSTERS

6. King Kong

1. A	2. C	3. A	4. A	5. C
6. C	7. C	8. A	9. D	10. A
11. A	12. A	13. C	14. A	15. A
16. B	17. B	18. D	19. A	20. B

7. The Wolfman & the Mummy

1. B	2. D	3. B	4. B	5. B
6. A	7. B	8. B	9. B	10. B
11. A	12. A	13. A	14. B	15. C
16. A	17. C	18. A	19. C	20. C

8. The Phantom of the Opera & the Hunchback of Notre Dame

1. A	2. D	3. C	4. C	5. A
6. A	7. A	8. C	9. A	10. B
11. C	12. A	13. A	14. C	15. B
16. C	17. A	18. A	19. A	20. C

9. Dr. Jekyll & the Invisible Man

1. C	2. A	3. A	4. A	5. D
6. A	7. A	8. A	9. A	10. B
11. C	12. C	13. A	14. C	15. A
16. B	17. C	18. D	19. B	20. B

10. Godzilla & Company

1. C	2. A	3. D	4. C	5. C
6. A	7. C	8. A	9. C	10. A
11. A	12. A	13. B	14. B	15. C
16. C	17. D	18. C	19. D	20. C

III THE NEXT GENERATION: ALIENS, DEMONS & BLOBS

11. Gore Galore

1. C	2. D	3. D	4. A	5. D
6. A	7. C	8. B	9. C	10. C
11. B	12. C	13. A	14. A	15. B
16. A	17. C	18. D	19. A	20. B

12. Midnight Madness

1. A	2. B	3. C	4. D	5. D
6. C	7. D	8. A	9. B	10. D
11. D	12. C	13. A	14. B	15. C
16. C	17. C	18. B	19. A	20. C

13. Prowlers & Howlers

1. A	2. C	3. A	4. B	5. B
6. B	7. B	8. D	9. C	10. B
11. B	12. D	13. A	14. D	15. B
16. A	17. A	18. B	19. D	20. C

14. TV Terror

1. A	2. B	3. A	4. D	5. C
6. B	7. D	8. C	9. A	10. A
11. B	12. B	13. B	14. B	15. A
16. B	17. A	18. A	19. A	20. A

15. Blood & Thud

1. C	2. D	3. D	4. B	5. D
6. D	7. C	8. B	9. D	10. D
11. A	12. B	13. A	14. A	15. B
16. A	17. C	18. B	19. D	20. D

16. Splatter & Shatter

1. B	2. B	3. A	4. C	5. B
6. A	7. A	8. B	9. A	10. A
11. B	12. B	13. C	14. D	15. C
16. C	17. D	18. B	19. C	20. A

17. Muck & Yuck

1. A	2. A	3. D	4. D	5. A
6. D	7. B	8. D	9. D	10. B
11. C	12. D	13. C	14. D	15. D
16. C	17. B	18. A	19. C	20. A

IV FACT, FOLKLORE & FICTION

18. Monsters in Mythology

1. C	2. D	3. B	4. B	5. A
6. D	7. B	8. B	9. A	10. B
11. B	12. B	13. B	14. D	15. B
16. C	17. D	18. B	19. B	20. A

19. Werewolves & Vampires

1. A	2. C	3. D	4. D	5. B
6. B	7. B	8. D	9. D	10. A
11. B	12. B	13. B	14. B	15. A
16. A	17. A	18. B	19. C	20. A

20. Mysterious Mummies

1. D	2. B	3. D	4. B	5. D
6. B	7. A	8. C	9. B	10. B
11. B	12. B	13. C	14. B	15. B
16. B	17. A	18. D	19. B	20. B

21. Witchery in History

1. A	2. D	3. D	4. D	5. C
6. D	7. D	8. D	9. C	10. C
11. C	12. D	13. A	14. C	15. B
16. C	17. A	18. B	19. B	20. B

22. Shudders from Shakespeare

1. B	2. B	3. A	4. B	5. A
6. B	7. C	8. B	9. C	10. A
11. D	12. D	13. C	14. C	15. B
16. D	17. A	18. D	19. C	20. B

23. Frightening Fiction

1. D	2. D	3. D	4. C	5. D
6. D	7. D	8. B	9. B	10. B
11. A	12. B	13. D	14. B	15. A
16. B	17. A	18. B	19. B	20. A

24. Scary Stories

1. D	2. C	3. B	4. D	5. D
6. C	7. B	8. B	9. A	10. A
11. A	12. D	13. D	14. B	15. A
16. C	17. B	18. B	19. D	20. D

INDEX

123

ABOUT THE AUTHOR

Dr. Arthur Liebman, Ph.D., is the author and editor of more than a dozen works of mystery and detective fiction, including award-winning books on Sherlock Holmes and the history of detective fiction. He has taught graduate and undergraduate courses in mystery, detective and Gothic literature at Stony Brook, Hofstra, and Adelphi Universities. A member of the Baker Street Irregulars, Dr. Liebman is currently on the faculty of two of New York's most prestigious schools: The New School for Social Research, where his popular courses in Sherlock Holmes, Agatha Christie and Dracula draw hundreds of students each year; and the American Academy of Dramatic Arts, the oldest school of drama in the English-speaking world, where he is Professor of Theatre and Film History.

In addition to teaching and writing, Dr. Liebman and his wife, Joyce, a concert pianist, appear often at colleges, libraries, and museums, as well as aboard luxury cruise ships, presenting their popular "music-with-mystery" show, "An Evening with Sherlock Holmes."

The Liebmans also conduct an annual tour of England in which they visit cities and sites associated with Sherlock Holmes, Agatha Christie, and Count Dracula.

The Liebmans have one son, Robert. They live in Roslyn Heights, New York.